SUCK IT UP
Memoirs of a Gym Mom

Lora Coad

Copyright © 2010 LLH Publishing
Cover Design by Gregg Coad

Please direct sales inquiries to:
CreateSpace: www.createspace.com/3491547
Amazon.com: www.amazon.com/dp/145388081X
LLH Publishing: llhpublishing.webs.com

This edition is printed and bound in the United States
by CreateSpace, a division of Amazon.com

To Svetlana
For making a difference

— suck it up
: to make the effort required to do or deal with something difficult or unpleasant

INTRODUCTION

Even in the womb, Kimberly was highly active, and from a young age I suspected she would become an athlete. Having no athletic tendencies or experience of my own, I anticipated many challenges. In reality, I found myself unprepared for the challenges. The road that Kimberly's athleticism took us down turned out to be an unforgettable test of character – for both of us. The experience gave Kimi strength, determination, resiliency and an adaptability that inspires me to this day. The experience taught me that sometimes life's greatest rewards come through dealing with something difficult.

Kimberly discovered her talent and passion for gymnastics at a very young age. Once that passion was ignited, no other activity could satisfy her so completely. In addition to passion, my daughter possessed natural ability, and her coaches recognized it right away. Her passion and talent led to big dreams, but she had a few lessons to learn along the way. After she learned the lesson of work ethic, she achieved a State Championship; but before she had a chance to pursue her ultimate goal, her dreams were shattered by a debilitating bone disorder.

Through all of the difficult lessons and challenges, Kimi pursued gymnastics with fervor. In spite of agony and injury along the way, she remained passionate and dedicated to her goal. She soldiered on until the day the doctor told her she had to quit. Even then, she saw no reason to cry in the face of adversity.

I, on the other hand, discovered many reasons to cry while on this journey. Because she is my daughter, I wanted to share her passion for gymnastics; I really did. However, I simply couldn't. The best I could offer was joy in seeing her happy. It was easy in the beginning because I had no idea what we'd gotten ourselves into. But as time wore on, I barely tolerated her sport and all its trappings. Outwardly, I supported her with a smile. Inwardly, I wished she would become enamored with spelling bees, or something I could relate to. When it came time to help her through the challenges that distress child athletes, I developed great anxiety. When it came time to mother her after an injury or chauffeur her to physical therapy, I almost despised the sport.

I don't know when or how, but I eventually learned to appreciate gymnastics. I began to value the sport for its contributions to our development – as individuals and as mother-daughter. I realized that Kimberly developed skills, learned dedication, and experienced a joy that many girls only dream of. In addition, I acquired new skills and felt joy through supporting her. My effort in learning to deal with something unnatural gave me insight into my own character in competitive settings. I am now more at ease with the notion of children-as-athletes. I can happily share stories of my daughter on the podium, beaming with pride. I developed greater admiration for gymnastics through our journey.

As mother and daughter, I believe we have learned to support each other because of our gymnastics experience. To this day Kimberly reflects on her days as a gymnast, and that reflection generates great conversations. We talk about her dreams and ambitions. We discuss ways she might transfer some of her skills to other areas of her life, and she genuinely appreciates my interest. My daughter discovered as she matured, that her mother is a human being who struggles just like she does. She's learned that, although we differ in our admiration for her sport, it was a labor of love for us both. And she understands that I shared her heartaches and joys every step of the way.

"And if you should ever wonder
How the years and you'll survive
Honey, you've got a mother who sings to you
Dances on the strings for you
Opens her heart and brings to you
An honest lullaby."
Joan Baez

EMERGENCE

"And so the hopping began . . ."

"Are you sure?" he asked, his face getting paler with every count.

We were recording the number of kicks I felt during a thirty minute period. The evidence told us that we were about to deliver a highly active baby. To be precise, our baby was ten times more active than the norm. Of course, I felt no surprise. I had carried the little darling around in my uterus for months, and the doctor had tested me for twins! She was bursting to get out. With every kick, my husband, Gregg, became more aware of the reality.

One endless month later, the big day arrived, or so we thought. I went into labor during Lamaze class, and our instructor sent us straight to the hospital, at which point the contractions stopped. A week later, the labor returned. I took my time calling Gregg, and we waited a few hours before going to the hospital. Once again the contractions came to an abrupt halt. As soon as we arrived home, they started up. It was as if the baby had already learned how to toy with us.

We waited through the night to be sure the labor was real. As an extra precaution, we went for a walk the next morning. Upon returning home to shower, the contractions stopped. The cycle repeated itself for four days. In response to desperate and exhaustive pleading, my doctor finally admitted me into the hospital. Our baby girl emerged that afternoon and lay peacefully under a heat lamp – in frog position.

And so the hopping began! It took all three of us (Mom, Dad, and big brother Cody) to keep up with Kimberly. From the day she entered our world, she hated restraint and she would not rest. She screamed bloody murder every time we put her in the car seat. She wanted – no, needed – constant stimulation. Sleep was not on her agenda. We were usually way beyond the point of exhaustion before she finally acquiesced at bed time.

1

As Kimberly grew, so did her need for continuous motion. According to the research, babies have over 600 distinguishable muscles. (Gesell and Ilg) I was sure she had more. All four of her limbs and every part in between were busy. We bought apparatus that rocked, bounced and swung. We strolled her, rolled her, and tossed her in the air ... until her gross motor skills developed and she began to do all of these things for herself. Then the real fun began.

My daughter was fearless; she climbed everything. If she couldn't climb it, she would swing or jump from it. In the absence of something to jump from, she rolled around on the furniture or made her dolls jump and roll. She even tortured the family cats into acrobatic feats that defied the imagination. One day, I sat working at my computer beneath the landing to the second story of our home. Kimi played overhead with a collection of cats and dolls – the higher the better. Suddenly, I found myself jolted by what felt like a ten pound bag of sugar landing on my head! I saw it out of the corner of my eye, scrambling off in terror to the farthest reaches of the room. The family cat, with some assistance from the family toddler, could indeed do flips in mid-air and still land on all fours. My daughter sat up on her perch looking satisfied while the rest of the family laughed hysterically from the sofa. The sofa – a place I rarely saw my daughter.

Kimberly only sat to read books with me when the plot involved action. She found acrobatics especially mesmerizing. Her favorite book was <u>Where the Wild Things Are</u>. A group of motley looking monsters swinging from trees always brought a smile to her face. Her favorite passage? "Let the wild rumpus start!"

As for watching television, Kimberly especially enjoyed ice skating and stopped dead in her tracks when it appeared. One might imagine a dainty little girl delicately pirouetting around the room in tandem to classical music. Not my pixie! She practiced her leaps and rolls. She imitated male skaters who could do back flips on the ice. She begged to stay up past her bedtime watching and mimicking, only to wake up the next morning and start over. She often turned the marital bed into her own personal practice arena.

One morning, Kimberly came leaping in at the crack of dawn. There was never any warning. She just arrived with a huge thump. On this particular morning, the thumping came as a back-beat to her sing-song voice. "Wake up, wake up! The birds are up and everything!" It was the weekend – my only day to catch a few extra winks. Extra winks? No such luck.

Her father escorted her downstairs where the furniture used to be. After numerous bouts of Kimberly's experiments in interior design, we just gave in and permanently rearranged things to accommodate her energy. She practiced her acrobatics on the living room floor every day. I looked forward to the day she could start preschool. They would have more structured activities, and we would get our house back. I counted the days until my little whirling dervish turned two.

The first day of preschool finally arrived and, thinking it a traumatic event, the entire family tagged along. Kimberly was barely two years old and small for her age. The children played outside as we entered the building. To our surprise, my daughter quickly wiggled her hands free and ran to the tallest climbing structure, scaling it to the highest peak. Her petite stature and acrobatic feat alarmed us all. I stood agape. Gregg stood agape. Big brother, Cody, chuckled. The teachers looked on, dumbfounded.

Within a week, Kimberly's teacher wisely recommended that we enroll her in an enrichment program for gross motor skills. We quickly agreed, and Kimi started "dance" the following week. She thoroughly enjoyed it, and the instructor enjoyed having her in class, probably because of her enthusiasm. Or, maybe it was the outfits she wore.

What outfits? My daughter hated clothing. During the first year of her preschool tenure, we battled daily to get her dressed in the morning. Shoes were merely toys, usually worn on the hands. Almost as fast as I put them on her feet, they would disappear. To keep me from putting them back on her little toes, she would hide them. As for clothing, she only wanted to wear a bathing suit and nothing more. Every day I put her clothes out only to find her running around the house in her swimsuit. I pleaded, chased, and tried to change her myself. But Kimi was a force to contend with. I soon realized the futility of my efforts.

One victorious morning, I discovered a bathing suit in Kimberly's lunch box as we arrived in the school parking lot. That was the last straw! I scolded her as we entered the building and, shamefully, the director overheard us. I noticed her questioning gaze as I headed for the door after delivering my little darling to her classroom.

"Uh, I guess you heard," I volunteered.

"Tough morning?" she responded.

"Aren't they all? She refuses to wear clothes. Every day it's the same thing," I explained. "All she wants to wear is her bathing suit. We go round and round. It's like a scene from a Tom and Jerry cartoon at my house in the morning."

We chuckled and then the wise preschool director offered a solution. "Why not just let her wear the bathing suit? We don't care."

"Seriously?" I hadn't considered that an option, but what a perfect way to end the morning clash!

From that day on, Kimberly wore bathing suits to school. We had nice light wash loads and no fights to start the day. It seemed much of my daughter's early life served as a precursor to the life ahead of us – one filled with acrobatics and scanty uniforms.

RESEARCH AND REFLECTION

I studied Child Development and understood the motor stages of infancy. I also knew something about the relationship between activity and intelligence. According to the experts, movements inside the womb indicate how active a person becomes after birth. More active the neonates tend to be more active individuals throughout life. "The total amount of activity which takes place during the fetal period is considerable; and if we had the requisite information we should find that this activity is already predictive of certain motor characteristics which the child will display in later life." (Gesell and Ilg, p. 225) In our case, Kimi's prenatal gymnastics certainly served as a precursor to later activity.

I welcomed Kimberly's active nature because I knew that babies learn through movement. Movement facilitates intellectual development and may even have an effect on all future intellectual growth. Intellectual stimulation then promotes further movement. It's a reciprocal relationship. (Payne) Through this understanding, I expected my daughter to be an intelligent child. Yet, I also wondered if her extreme activity level might imply a future diagnosis of ADHD.

When Kimi's constant state of motion failed to calm after a few years, my worry intensified. By eighteen months she climbed out of her crib and negotiated the stairs as if they were a mere bump in the road. At twenty to twenty-two months she climbed over the railing of the stairs when left unattended. By two years of age, she scaled the entertainment center. By the time she was three years old, she stacked coffee tables and then scrambled atop her construction. I was a child care professional, yet I had very little experience with this type of behavior. Was it normal?

After nine years of working in a preschool, I was familiar with normal physical development in small children. Children's motor control improves drastically at two years. Gross motor skills develop to the point that they can climb over almost anything. They move with confidence and mastery, a reflection not only of motor ability but also of a greater sense of self. (Brazelton and Greenspan) I'd seen children climb over tables and learn to master the playground apparatus. I'd just never seen a brand new two-year old scale the tallest climbing structure on the first day of school. I'd definitely never seen a tiny little girl behave in such a manner. Boys were more likely to exhibit advanced motor skills at the age of two.

There is a reason why boys might be more likely to tackle climbing structures on the first day of preschool. "The female brain is coded to secrete more serotonin than the male. Higher serotonin secretion is directly related to greater impulse control. This is why one-or two-or three year old girls will tend to be physically calmer than the same-age boy," (Gurian, p. 33) and "his brain is more dominant in the right hemisphere, giving him less sensory and more spatial perspective. He fidgets, moves around, tries to throw things, tries to jump, and walks earlier than girls." (Gurian, p. 34) Fascinating. Kimberly had the behavioral characteristics of a boy. I wondered if that meant she was destined to become an athlete.

I found having an athletically inclined daughter to be desirable. Girls who develop gross motor skills early in life usually fare well academically, and studies have shown that girls who participate in sports have better self-esteem. (Harmel, 1998) Therefore, parenting an active little girl gave me optimism about her future potential. Kimi's athletic inclination meant she could become a successful, self-assured student. I secretly hoped she might become the first woman in our family to earn a PhD.

Yet, there was a pang of doubt somewhere inside me. She seemed more than just "a little bit" athletic. She acted more like Forrest Gump – someone who could start running and just keep going, for no good reason at all. I worried about what sort of relationship the two of us might develop as my little girl grew. I was a bookworm and avoided the challenge of relating to athletic females. I am the type of person who prefers harmony to competition and, I always felt uncomfortable with rivalry. I was unsure about the skills I might need in her future world.

DISCOVERY

"Her daily ambition was to climb and release, falling into the foam pit below."

"So you're Kimi's mom!" she exclaimed as I approached. "Are you going to put her in competition?"

"Wait! Stop the train!" I thought, "She's only five year's old."

We'd just witnessed a modest little demonstration that didn't exactly prepare me for the coach's enthusiasm. I must have been standing there with a look of disbelief.

Sensing my apprehension, the coach quickly added: "It's just that she's really talented." She then offered her hand and introduced herself, "I'm Sherrie Villanueva."

"Lora," I responded as we shook hands. "Kimberly is really enjoying herself, and she seems to like you a lot."

Just then, the topic of conversation came bounding up with her father in tow. "This is my husband, Gregg," I said.

As they shook hands, I turned to my daughter. "Sherrie says you're doing a great job in her class. Let's take a picture."

Wow, I thought! Three years since she scaled the climbing structure on her first day of preschool and she still had so much energy. I was happy to hear that, at least outside the house, she had a healthy outlet. At home it continued to be a constant effort to keep her off the furniture.

Almost every day I heard her father yell, "Kimi, save that for the gym!" or "Get off your head; you're going to break your neck!"

I wondered whether she was practicing a trick she learned in gymnastics or inventing a new one. Knowing how much she enjoyed the extra-curricular activity made me happy, for she was definitely a child full of life. And she found a satisfying channel for that vigor. Kindergarten was a good year.

Then came summer and, in spite of her enjoyment of gymnastics, Kimi was still mesmerized by skating. She wanted to take to the ice. The costumes, the movements and the speed with which athletes moved around a rink captivated her. She ran to the television any time she heard the *whoosh* of blades scraping the ice. She watched intently as skaters executed twists, turns, jumps, lifts, and throws. She longed for skates of her own. So, during that summer after kindergarten, I enrolled her in an introductory class at the local rink. After years of built up anticipation, she was overly excited. And, after such success and aptitude for gymnastics, she also had lofty expectations.

As it turned out, reality didn't quite match the dream. She had envisioned a different experience. She found the ice frigid, the skates cumbersome, and the coaches less than enthusiastic about her aptitude. I bought gloves, leggings and headbands. However, all of the additional layers proved to be a major inconvenience. As she complained about being cold, I wondered if she'd imagined skating in her bathing suit. The skates were heavy, clumsy, foreign objects that impeded her progress. "They weigh my feet down," she explained. I wondered if she'd rather wear them on her hands. My daughter could not conceive of using shoes as a tool. Yes, she proved awkward on the ice and, in this arena, she failed to get special attention for her athletic prowess. It turned out to be too much for her to accept. On the way home from class one day, she initiated a conversation with me about her experience.

"I want to go back to gymnastics," she declared.

"Really?" I asked, as I wondered what she was thinking.

"Yeah, I think God gave me more of a gift for that than ice skating," she responded.

God? I thought. And barely able to hide my amusement, I said, "Well, it doesn't matter to me. You just need to choose something that helps you keep the wiggles out during school hours. School starts soon, so if you're serious, we'll sign you up."

"I'm serious," she replied.

A few weeks later, the year commenced, and so did gymnastics. About a month later, however, Kimberly suddenly declared that she hated it and never wanted to go again. I felt a bit frustrated and wasn't immediately sure how to respond. After some consideration, I decided extra-curricular activities should be fun and pulled her from the class. I also began looking for another sport. She simply required it. At the age of five, my daughter still didn't sleep through the night, and the condition worsened with less activity. After a week of no extra recreation, she was literally outside herself.

I wondered whether she could take sleeping pills at the young age of six. Yes, I seriously considered knocking her out with drugs at that point. I had gone years without a solid night's sleep, and I needed eight uninterrupted hours. I longed for a bed without her climbing up into it. I wanted a morning without her waking me up before the roosters crowed. I considered a lock on my bedroom door.

"Right," I thought, "she'll find a way through the locked door to torture me."

For a while, we continued our routine – Kimberly waking us up followed by an escort back to bed – except on those nights when her father and I were simply too tired. On those nights, I chose bruised ribs over collapsing on the floor in a failed attempt at returning her to bed.

"When will she find a way to turn her mind and body off at night?" I wondered, "Why the sudden dislike for gymnastics? What will we do now to keep her busy?"

Luckily, a few weeks later I learned the reason for Kimi's sudden dislike for gymnastics. Brittany, one of the older girls in the program, was a classmate Kimberly's brother, Cody. Brittany approached me after school one day to chat. In the course of the conversation I learned my daughter wasn't the only one to quit. Sherrie was no longer coaching. A replacement had been hired and, it seemed the younger children weren't working well with the new coach.

I quickly thought of a solution to our dilemma; the neighborhood YMCA had a gymnastics program. Excited about the prospect of finding Kimberly another outlet for her pent-up energy, I asked if she would like to go to a different gym – one with children her age and nice coaches. She was excited at the suggestion, so we enrolled her within a week.

The YMCA offered a different form of gymnastics and I was nervous. The school sponsored program had limited equipment. It had focused on acrobatics and pyramids, so the students used mats, geometric foam structures and each other. The YMCA had an artistic program, equipped with traditional bars, beams, vaults, spring floors and trampolines. I worried that Kimberly might not adjust to the transition.

My worries proved to be unfounded. Kimi was awestruck! She loved the new equipment, the adoring coaches, and the other girls. The main attraction, a rope that hung from the ceiling, became her new obsession. My daughter wanted nothing more than to climb and release, falling into the foam pit below. The coaches enjoyed her fearlessness, and she loved to accommodate them. She constantly attempted more daring feats and worked diligently to perfect new skills. Best of all, the other girls shared her energy. They ran and tumbled together. They laughed and played together. It was organized chaos, in my mind. In her mind, everybody was there for a single purpose – challenging each other to unimaginable feats. She was in her element. It seemed a strange, but desperately needed place.

Kimberly found a new outlet for her excess energy, and I breathed a sigh of relief. I felt increasingly optimistic about the prospect of getting her to sleep at night. We went on with our daily lives – work, school, gymnastics, and, oh yes, wrestling. Cody started high school that year and the wresting coach recruited him for the team. We spent our weekends following his tournaments and little sister had a new audience to perform for. Thank God it was in a gym!

My daughter's splits, tumbling and handstands entertained crowds almost as much as the wrestling. The team called her their mascot. Other teams and parents stared in awe. She relished it. I resigned myself to it. I knew her agenda could never include sitting quietly by my side – reading, coloring or stringing beads like other little girls.

RESEARCH AND REFLECTION

When Kimberly experienced frustration with ice skating, I had no problem allowing her to resign. Some parents might wonder if permitting a child to quit something she's started is advisable. After all, children develop self-esteem through accomplishment, and the process of becoming better includes failure. (Zimmerman) Was my decision to let her quit an indulgence? Was it ill-advised? At five years old, her spatial awareness should be fully developed, and her directional awareness should be developing. She should be able to skate, right?

Wrong. At five years old the temporal awareness required for complex synchronous movement is not yet developed. (Payne) It was simply impossible for Kimi to perform as an ice skater at that age. The best she could hope for was to keep her ankles straight, her butt off the ice, and glide from one end of the rink to the other – maybe backwards sometimes. Because of her gymnastics experience, she had a completely different expectation and very little patience for the natural progression of learning this new skill.

Developmentally, it was also appropriate for Kimberly to be pragmatic about gymnastics versus ice skating (Gesell and Ilg). I was neither surprised nor disappointed by the announcement that she wished to return to gymnastics. Five year-olds prefer to function within their range of capabilities. They prefer stability, and it is for this reason that they exude a greater sense of competence than they do at four years of age. Kimi exhibited typical behavior, and normal behavior was fine with me. At that point, I preferred to manage her on the basis of her sense of self-limits. I believed it would be ill-advised to challenge her beyond her limitations at her age. More importantly, we were considering an extra-curricular activity. I merely wanted to satiate her need for physical activity. Furthermore, I had an acquaintance who'd been a professional ice skater. She warned me about the financial black hole that ice skating could become should Kimberly pursue the sport. I felt relief when Kimberly decided against it without my influence. I figured we had plenty of time for lessons in perseverance.

THE GIFT

".... her gymnastics dream and some unimaginable trick she mastered."

She turned and looked me in the eyes and said emphatically, "No, you don't understand, she's really good."

A few months had passed at the new gym and I was discussing Kimberly's latest promotion with her coach. We were happy she had found a satisfying outlet for her energy and relieved that she was finally sleeping better. She liked the new gym, appeared to be thriving in their program, and asked if she could add another day of classes. We agreed to two days each week for one to one and a half hours a day. Apparently, she was not alone in the satisfaction of added time at the gym. The coaches appreciated her eagerness to learn, her athletic prowess and her fearlessness. She moved ahead quickly, mastered skills and looked for new challenges every day.

Yet all the time Kimi spent at the gym came with a price. It seemed gymnastics was practically all she thought about. I felt deprived of my little girl, and I missed her. The gym benefited from her zest for life. I wanted to experience those benefits at home. Our special times together diminished. We had increasingly less time for dress up, tea parties and outdoor adventures. At night she returned home late, and we realized less time to read together before bedtime. The bedtime routine became calmer, but she still found sleep to be distasteful. Sleep was not on her agenda – not until she started dreaming about gymnastics.

Kimi woke up at least once a week retelling the story of her gymnastics dream and some unimaginable trick she mastered. Either that or she drew pictures to show us. On one such occasion, she arose to share her dream of the Olympics. Of course, she won the gold on every event. They even named a new trick after her. She drew a picture of herself on the podium, medals weighing her down and flowers surrounding her countenance. I thought it was the cutest thing I'd ever seen and decided to share it with her coach. When my daughter found out, she screamed in humiliation.

"You *GAVE* him my picture!" she yelled in disbelief.

"I thought he would like it. It's a way to show how much you appreciate everything he teaches you," I explained.

"I don't want him to know about my dreams," she said.

"Why not?" I inquired.

"Because it's embarrassing. Doesn't every little gymnast have the same dream? He'll think it's stupid," she whispered, shame in her small voice.

"Oh. I'm sorry, I didn't think of it that way," I apologized. I really was sorry. And I thought she was beyond her years in maturity.

Following that episode, Kimberly progressed quickly in gymnastics. For whatever reason, the dreams and subsequent discussions seemed to spawn greater determination within her. Maybe it was her age. She was seven years old, an age when children typically set goals too high for themselves. (Gesell and Ilg). At any rate, my daughter suddenly became more serious about advancement. A few months later, she was one level away from the coveted "gold" group she desired. The gold group trained for competition. She had only one skill remaining in order to qualify – a front hip circle on bars. I had no idea what a front hip circle was, but I knew that for some unknown reason, it did not come as easily to her as prior skills had. Instead of mastering it in one or two lessons, it took five or six. She felt frustrated, but what tenacity she displayed!

For the first time, I watched Kimberly "suck it up" to master that skill. Suck it up? She hadn't even heard the expression, and we certainly never used it. Yet, somehow, she already understood it was part of the gymnastics culture. Outside a military setting, I hated the concept. Sucking it up was something one does to get through an undesirable situation, like living in trenches while fighting a war. Gymnastics should be the opposite of undesirable.

Watching her struggle with a difficult and unnecessary physical accomplishment struck me as stressful for a first grader. I wanted to fall apart at the seams in my empathy for her, but she was in her element. When she finally learned the front hip circle, she felt proud. I'd never seen her more self-satisfied, and I learned the first of many lessons as the mother of an athlete.

Through witnessing Kimi's struggle, I learned that self-esteem comes with hard work and accomplishment, even for a little girl. I learned that my instinct to protect her from that struggle came from fear – fear that she might fail. I also understood that if she did fail, she would learn the process of improvement. I had to let her struggle. I learned my job as her mother was not to protect her from failure or struggle, but to support her through it. I learned to sit patiently and watch while she worked hard to get herself over the bars, mastering that skill.

Soon, Kimberly was attending gym three days a week and learning to compete. We received a phone call asking us if they could test her for a special class. Already suspecting what the answer would be, we decided to ask her what she wanted. As we expected, she answered with a resounding "yes!" By summer Kimi started asking if she could go to gym every day. I felt caught up in something frightening – something that involved losing my daughter. It was a bittersweet pain, though. I missed her and wanted more time with her, but I also felt lucky to share life with her. My small daughter showed ambition and thrived on challenge. She found passion in life, and she was having more fun than I could have given her without gymnastics.

That summer, Kimberly spent her mornings in training and her afternoons at the pool with her gym buddies and other YMCA kids. When the coaches offered demonstrations, they invited her to participate. She went to the mall and had her pictures taken with other gymnasts. She felt special. On the weekends, she went to open gym – a day of free play on the equipment. She went to other girls' houses for pool parties and sleepovers. As a group, they gathered to watch elite gymnasts perform on television. They each believed they could be just like those girls one day. My daughter shared big dreams with small girls and, to her, the dream was real. The possibility of her ever realizing that dream seemed remote to me.

Kimi was only in second grade, but she practiced diligently and learned new skills every month. It was a year of preparation and hard work. During this time I began to see how passionate she was. The gym hosted a demonstration for parents and, of course, we took our video camera to document the big event. Advanced performances followed the young girls' demonstration. Kimi insisted on staying to watch and film. We looked for a suitable place to sit, but the gym was crowded. We resorted to standing in the back near one of her coaches.

In the middle of the presentation, Kimberly declared, "I want to live at the gym."

Her coach chuckled and piped in with, "Gee, Kimi, I think there are a few things you still need your parents for."

"Like what?" she asked.

It was my turn. "Oh, food, clothes, a ride to school, and money for other things you like to do – like go to Disneyland."

She wasn't going to settle for that answer. She took about a half a minute to figure it out and offered up her solution. "I know! You can pick me up in the morning, bring food and a change of clothes, drop me off at school, then pick me up in the afternoon and bring me back. They have a mini-fridge, a freezer, and a microwave here. I can sleep on the mats – or in the pit! I'll be fine, Mom."

"Okay, I guess I know where I fit in her list priorities," I whispered to her coach, as we chuckled some more.

I resigned myself to standing in support of my daughter's passion as the day progressed. I studied her as she looked on in awe at the team demonstrations. Silently, I wondered if my daughter understood the ramifications of what she had suggested. I tried to figure out how I could deal with my own feelings of rejection. I struggled to suppress my true emotions. I knew Kimi was just a little girl and probably didn't completely realize how ludicrous an idea it was to live at the gym. I also knew how fiercely independent she was and how little she needed me. I peered longingly at a mother in the seat ahead of us cuddling her baby girl and wondered what I did do deserve this plight. At that moment, I wanted to snatch my daughter up and run away from the hot, crowded gym.

I didn't take her and run, and we soon learned that Kimberly qualified to compete in the fall. Along with a hefty price tag for team gear, coaching, and entry fees, came a bundle of excitement. The expense mattered little to Gregg and me, considering how hard she'd worked. My daughter's exuberance served as a contagion. Our baby was shaping up to be quite something, and we savored the moment. I think Gregg savored it a bit more whole-hardheartedly; however, since I knew I would continue to enjoy less time with my baby. Outwardly, I smiled, cheered and bragged to anyone who would listen – just so everyone would know I could perform in the role of supportive mom. Inwardly, I tried to convince myself it was all good. My daughter was unique and that was good. She had passion and that was good. Her athletic tendencies and talent would benefit her in other ways – all good. Right? Right. It was a happy time.

RESEARCH AND REFLECTION

Developmentally, seven year-olds should be more cautious in their approach to new performances. (Gesell and Ilg) I wondered why my daughter didn't exhibit any caution. Eight year-olds should suddenly demand more of their mother's attention. I especially wondered why Kimi didn't want more time with me. Once again, my daughter proved to be an enigma.

The only behavior Kimi exhibited at this age that matched expert predictions was a sense of seriousness. According to Gesell and Ilg, eight year-olds set up high goals, want to be perfect and show pride in their abilities. They are persistent, avid and conscientious. They are ready to face new challenges and readily go out of bounds. Exactly true in my daughter's case. However, this has always been true for Kimberly. How could I trust it to be a developmental phase? And, if it wasn't just a phase, what could I do about it? I was constantly at a loss trying to balance my daughter's intense ambition, independent nature, and developmental phases. She kept me on my toes. And she kept me wondering when we might be able to squeeze some family time into her busy schedule.

Brazelton and Greenspan advise time with parents every day for healthy child development. Time should include opportunities to talk so that children might negotiate challenges and learn to master skills. I knew this, and I wanted it. I tried to make opportunities where none existed. We talked in the car. We were still following her brother's wrestling tournaments, so I tried to capitalize on that time as well. However, she continued to fidget and entertain the crowd at tournaments. She didn't want to sit and talk with me.

She could not stop herself from practicing – possibly for good reason. A fascinating part of the brain, the hippocampus, becomes developed in girls at seven or eight years old, giving her the ability to remember. It also operates at great speed, giving girls complex memory function and greater storage capacity than boys. This change in brain function played a part in Kimi's gymnastics skills. In her own mind, she had to continue practicing. And practice makes perfect.

She wanted to be perfect in order to accomplish the goal of success. I knew she must also have sport-specific knowledge, skills and movement execution. "Raw athletic ability does not necessarily ensure athletic success." (Payne and Isaacs, p. 37) She needed time at the gym to accomplish her goal. But more time at the gym meant less time with us. It was an ongoing dilemma.

As Kimi's time at the gym continually increased, my sense that her childhood had somehow taken an abnormal direction haunted me. And it wasn't just the time at the gym that bothered me. She also seemed to spend increased mental energy in pursuit of her passion. I felt a duty to create a bond with my daughter and then gradually dissolve it as she grew. She seemed to care little of our bond. Everything in our relationship ran contrary to the book of life. Instead of gradually moving toward a state of separation, it seemed our relationship was born into separation. I had no experience in this area. I neither knew anyone with such a child, nor had I studied the phenomenon. I floundered in unfamiliar territory. I desperately wanted to offer her both a healthy family environment as well as an opportunity to satisfy her ambition, but I was at a loss.

INFATUATION OR TRUE LOVE?

Her tears were a response to the sorrow and fear she felt in knowing I might make her quit ....

I was forty-five miles away when I got the call from Kimberly's coach informing me that my daughter was hurt. She had fallen while practicing a double back-hand spring, and they thought she had broken her arm. They tried to contact my husband, Gregg, and couldn't reach him. Panic struck. I was in the middle of something important at work that required my presence. How could I leave? How could I stay? Even if I did leave, I felt tortured knowing it would be at least an hour until I got to her. Guilt set in. A good mother would be there sooner. No need to question whether or not I would go to her.

I began making arrangements at work to get to Kimberly as soon as possible. It was early evening, so I also called the insurance company to figure out proper procedures for after hour care. Just as I was getting into the car, my cell phone rang. Finally! It was Gregg, equally panicked. The coaches found him and he was at the gym, but he didn't know what to do. He asked me where to take our daughter at such a late hour. I gave instructions, told him I would be there as soon as possible and then asked how she was doing.

"She's fine," my husband said, "... not a tear. She's just sitting here with ice on her elbow. I'll see you at the hospital."

A day later, my baby underwent surgery at the ripe young age of eight. What a nightmare. She'd broken her elbow at the growth plate. However, she approached the trauma as if it were just another day. She acted like there was no pain involved. The day after surgery, she had visitors and cards from the gym. She maintained a sunny disposition and promised she would be back in time to compete. On day three, she seemed somehow more reserved. Upon closer examination, I learned the cause. Post-operative pain had set in. On the one hand, I shared her pain. On the other hand, I felt somewhat thankful that reality finally hit. Recognizing a rare opportunity, I approached the object of my affection gingerly.

There she lay in silence with three pins sticking through the wrapping. Feeling both sympathetic and sick to my stomach, I seriously wanted her to give up this dangerous sport. But it was just one short week after qualifying to compete, so I knew her pain was punctuated by disappointment. I decided to capitalize on the moment.

"I'm so sorry you fell and broke your arm, baby," I said, as I tucked her in, changed her ice pack and administered pain medication. Then I wiped a single tear from her eye and added, "We should pray about this. Maybe gymnastics isn't the best sport for you."

She just lay there with more tears welling up in her eyes. Thinking she understood, and believing she agreed with me, I added, "Just look at all the injuries the champions have suffered over the years. This probably won't be the only time you'll get hurt." I was referring to the gymnasts she'd been watching on television that summer, and the announcers' constant recap of past injuries.

At that point, Kimi sat straight up in bed, declaring, "I'm fine." Once again, she was sucking it up. Damn!

It was then that I began to understand how deeply committed she was, how strong her spirit had grown, and how impossible it would be to separate her from the sport she loved. Her tears were a response to the sorrow and fear she felt in knowing I might make her quit gymnastics. And my tears, later that evening in solitude, were a response to the sorrow and fear I felt in knowing I couldn't make her quit. I wanted to make her quit, so I initiated a conversation with Gregg. The discussion was short, and it ended with me knowing the price would be too great. She was, after all, my daughter. Nobody could understand her like I could. I knew her spirit, and forcing her to quit would crush that spirit. Lest I forget, Gregg reminded me of that fact. He was a former athlete, and he could relate. I had to trust his judgment and cry in silence.

Determination punctuated Kimberly's behavior during the upcoming season. Even though she couldn't compete, my daughter never missed a workout. She dressed out and went to every meet, supporting her team with enthusiasm. I did not, could not, understand her insistence to behave in such a bizarre fashion. Furthermore, I'd been looking forward to her period of rehabilitation. I saw it as an opportunity to spend more time together – catch up on our reading and tea parties. No such luck. Kimberly's resilience preempted injury, and she had a tough exterior.

Only once, toward the end of the season, did I catch a glimpse of something soft inside my steadfast little eight-year old. As I entered the gym toward the end of practice, Kimi entered the parent viewing room. As she slowly approached me, I noticed a tear on her cheek.

She broke down when I asked, "What's wrong?"

"I'm just so tired of being on the sideline," she sobbed. Her crying lasted about two minutes. Then she sucked it up and went back out to the floor. Damn, I thought. She shares none of my DNA.

Several long weeks later, Kimberly's doctor finally gave the okay for her return to gymnastics. She was so excited that she insisted on going straight to the gym, where she could swing from the bars. Her frustration soon returned, however. She had lost muscle and strength in her arm. In response, my daughter developed an unexpected fear of the bars. Since her accident happened during floor exercises, it took me a while to figure it out. The bars require almost 100% use of the arms. Her arm was weak and she lost confidence in her ability to use it. At that point, she didn't understand that strength returns with use. It would take a year and the insight of a very special coach for her to regain confidence and the ability to perform on the bars again.

Meanwhile, we conducted family life as usual – with work, school and sports. However, in the aftermath of Kimberly's injury, I lived in constant fear for her safety. I often had conversations with myself about the decision to stick with gymnastics. I felt it was my parental duty to protect her; and, no matter how hard I tried, I failed to comprehend her daredevil ways. I barely tolerated the danger that she tempted, and prayed she would discover a different fascination. I wanted my daughter to choose books over gymnastics, but I had no control, and I felt helpless. Privately, I hated myself for the decision we made. Publicly, I maintained a sunny disposition. My public behavior reflected my forced state of determination. Like Kimi, I sucked it up.

RESEARCH AND REFLECTION

When Kimi injured herself at such a young age, I struggled with feelings of guilt and inadequacy. I didn't understand her desire to participate in such a dangerous sport. I wanted to change her world, but couldn't. Her strong will would not allow it. The experience tested me. I felt particularly at odds when it came time to explain to friends and family who wondered out loud whether gymnastics was such a good idea. I tried not to worry about what people thought, but worry I did. Doesn't every mother? Doesn't every mother want to be perceived as a good mother? I needed people to understand my impossible predicament, but I was ill-equipped to articulate the reasons behind my feelings and decisions. As Evelyn Bassoff so adeptly puts it in her book, Mothers and Daughters,

> "a *good* mother protects her child against life's hardness – its frustrations, losses and despair ... When they do not protect their daughters from the tragedies that are part of the human condition, these mothers are likely to suffer from guilt and frustration ... We have invested maternal love with an enormous amount of power – the power to save and the power to heal. A sweetly poisonous Victorian verse reminds us:

> *Don't poets know it better than others?*
> *God can't be everywhere: and so,*
> *Invented mothers."*

She goes on to say,

> "maternal power is illusory, and this illusion causes much unnecessary suffering. Not only does it lead to a sense of maternal inadequacy but, in some cases, to a sense of maternal destruction. For surely, if mothers believe they have the power to make their children happy, they will also believe that they have the power to bring about their children's ruination. In keeping with this belief, mothers hold themselves responsible – and are held responsible in the court of public opinion – for any number of afflictions ... that strike young people." (pp. 61- 62)

My feelings of inadequacy were punctuated by the realization that I just did not fit into Kimberly's gymnastics world. Once she reached the competitive level, I began to notice a striking difference in the behavior of some of the parents – mothers in particular. I group them with the stereotypical "soccer mom." They hung out in the gym watching their daughters almost daily. They knew and used technical terms for gymnastics skills – terms the average person doesn't understand. They compared gymnasts, critiqued the coaches and seemed to let their blood pressure rise over things they could not control.

I didn't have the time or the inclination to dwell on things I could not control. Yet, I wondered if this aspect of gymnastics was part of the culture. Was I expected to know the meaning of technical terms like kip, flick, straddle-back and pechanko? I feared the expectation of becoming part of the group. And I thought Kimi expected me to become part of the group. She started asking me to watch her work out more often. She wanted me at the gym sitting with the other moms. She begged if I resisted. She complained when I failed to show up. I spent this time vacillating between a strong desire to support my daughter and a loathing of what it involved. I didn't care about technical terms, avoided critique of coaches and, certainly didn't want to compare my daughter to the other girls. I knew I never wanted to become a gym mom in the stereotypical sense of the word.

Was I supposed to become a stereotypical gym mom and embrace the culture?" And exactly what is gym culture? According to Webster, culture is "the customary beliefs, social forms, and material traits of a racial, religious, or social group." We absorb cultural traditions and participate in them. We perpetuate them. Culture is sustained by people who pressure each other to conform. Non-conformists make followers feel uncomfortable. Rebels are made to feel unwelcome – tolerated maybe but not accepted. (Wiseman) There are rules for belonging (successfully) to a particular cultural group (see table on the next page).

Was my resistance to the gym culture a sign of rebellion? Did it mean I would not be accepted by the group? More importantly, what was behind my discomfort? In her book Queen Bee Moms & King Pin Dads, Rosalind Wiseman says parents feel uncomfortable participating in groups that focus on their children because

> "You feel like you're back in middle school. It's clear who's at the top of the social ladder, who's not, and who's waiting to climb up from the lower rings. You either want to be part of it or you don't. If you do, you hope to fit in well, be highly placed. If you don't, you may find yourself in a situation where you have no choice. By virtue of the fact that you are your child's parent, you already belong. Yet the dynamics of the group and the group culture may run counter to your beliefs. Being a member may come at the cost of the values you stand for."

It did seem like I was back in middle school and it was obvious who was at the top of the totem pole. It was ugly and I wanted no part of it, but I was in a situation where I had no choice. I had to support my daughter. So, I sucked it up.

RULES FOR BELONGING (SUCCESSFULLY) TO A PARTICULAR CULTURAL GROUP
Please the person in power
Maintain relationships with the people in power
Pleasing the people in power may result in an inability to say what you need or want
Loyalty means backing up your friends, even when their actions are unethical or cruel
Be silent in the face of cruelty, lest it be turned on you

Keeping the unspoken rules in mind, I committed myself to spending a few hours a week in the parent viewing room. I thought of it as an opportunity to spend more time with Kimberly – talk with her about negotiating challenges. I smiled and chatted with the other moms. Privately, I prayed the serenity prayer:

> *God grant me the Serenity*
> *To accept the things I cannot change*
> *The Power*
> *To change the things I can*
> *And the Wisdom*
> *To know the difference*

TRANSITIONS

"The day I took her to observe the new gym, my little reticent one was surprised...."

"No way!" she cried. "If you make me move, I'm quitting gymnastics!"

We had already decided to move Kimberly to a different gym. Being so far away on the day she broke her arm tortured me. Although it all worked out, I wanted to be able to get to her more quickly. Gregg and I each worked an hour away from the YMCA and in opposite directions. We agreed that she had to be closer to one of us, and I found a gym one block away from my office.

As we tried to explain the rationale behind moving her to a new gym, Kimberly emphatically refused to cooperate. As much as we hated to force the issue, the situation required an ultimatum. We had to call her bluff.

"Fine, quit," Gregg said. "You're done at the end of the month."

"But don't you want to at least go look at it?" I added.

Silence. Kimi was hurt, and when she was hurt, she was angry. When she was angry, she was stubbornly silent. But I believed stubbornness could work to her advantage later in life, and I had no desire to break her spirit. "Stubbornness in and of itself is not a bad trait. In fact, it may be one of her best assets if she learns to use it to her advantage." (Gadeberg, p. 122)

At a standstill, the discussion ended. Kimi needed time to think. Maybe we all needed time to think. As much as she loved her gym, I felt a pang of guilt at our decision.

Two days later, my daughter revisited the idea of change, saying, "Okay, I'll look at the new gym. But I'm only looking."

27

The day I took her to observe the new gym, my little reticent one showed surprise at seeing girls practicing familiar routines. I don't know what she expected, but I felt a puzzled relief. She found comfort in something that remained an enigma to me.

Immediately recognizing the difference in equipment, Kimi shared her surprise. "Their gym is huge!" she exclaimed. "Look at those cool trampolines, and they have so many beams!" Dreamily, she sighed, "Wow, two vaults." Vault was her favorite apparatus.

Apparently popular, the new gym had limited openings. Consequently, the coaching staff evaluated gymnasts before admitting them into the program. Since Kimberly warmed up to the idea of making a move, I called for a try-out. My daughter seemed nervous, but also excited on the day that she met with the coach. She still needed to improve her bar skills after the broken arm, but the coach accepted her into the program. Kimberly showed some lingering apprehension about the move, but her tension eased when she recognized a couple girls that she knew from the YMCA. She started at the new gym that same week.

At Kimi's urging, I agreed to stay at the gym with her on her first day. And her apprehension turned to excitement within an hour. While at the chalk bin, she came face to face with a well known elite gymnast who she'd seen on television. Her jaw dropped as she looked through the window into the viewing room at me. On the way home, she told me about the conversation she had with the same girl.

"You're in my way," Kimi said to the star gymnast who was on the same mat during floor exercises.

"You're new here, aren't you?" the girl replied.

Upon hearing this story, I laughed and thought it sounded exactly like something Kimi would do – so intently focused, she didn't even realize who she was talking to, or that she was slightly out of line.

In spite of the minor faux pax, it wasn't long before Kimi made friends with the girls at her new gym. They seemed charmed by her fun-loving ways. She went on outings, parties and sleepovers – things that hastened the transition and made her feel more accepted. Apparently, however, the coaching staff failed to appreciate her entertaining ways. This was a serious training center, and the coaches expected girls to treat their workout with respect. My little girl got into trouble for appearing to take things lightly.

I knew Kimberly only appeared to take things lightly. In reality, I thought, she took gymnastics far too seriously. My conflicted feelings left me unsure about how to proceed. On one hand, I wanted to provide her with whatever guidance she needed to be more successful; on the other hand, I thought it was silly for nine year-olds to be in the position of having to take an extra-curricular activity so seriously. I wanted her to know that she should decide what she wanted, and she needed to be able to do that without my opinion influencing her. I decided to have a carefully thought-out talk with her.

I wanted my daughter to continue finding joy in her sport, but I feared my influence might cause her fun-loving behavior to take a rebellious twist. My job was to support and guide her in the path of success, not rebellion. After careful consideration, I decided to philosophize about taking things seriously versus having fun. I hoped she could find a way to do both. What she needed was a new angle. "Provide children with what they don't get anywhere else: a new perspective." (Shelby and Smith, p. 79) The conversation we had on the way home that day went something like this.

"How do you feel about getting into trouble for having fun in the gym?" I asked.

"I don't like it," Kimberly replied.

"Is there any way you can have fun without getting into trouble?" I followed.

"I can't help it. I love gymnastics, and I get so excited," she answered.

"So why do you think the coaches get upset when girls have fun?" I inquired.

"I don't know," my daughter responded.

"I don't either," I added. "You should enjoy your sport, but maybe when you goof off it affects the other girls. There are safety concerns. The coaches are probably afraid somebody will get hurt."

I let some time pass as we drove and she snacked on her dinner. She almost always had to eat in the car after a late work-out.

A while later, I followed up with "What do you think?"

"I don't know," she answered with a puzzled look on her face. I feared the conversation was not headed in the right direction.

After some thought and a few more bites of food, her quick mind added, "Won't they kick me out if I don't do what they want?"

I responded by saying, "Maybe, I guess that is something you have to think about."

"Well," she retorted, "gymnastics is way too important. I guess I will just quit having so much fun."

My heart ached. And we both sucked it up.

RESEARCH AND REFLECTION

Making the transition to a new gym proved more challenging to me than to my daughter. The seriousness of the environment baffled me. I fought the urge to yell, "They are just children!" I wanted to ask more than one mother, "Why are you here? She clearly doesn't enjoy this."

Perplexed, I found myself, once again doubting every decision we made regarding Kimberly and gymnastics. When she got into trouble for her fun-loving ways during work-outs, I developed second thoughts about placing her in a serious training center, and even considered another change.

In the book, <u>Games Girls Play; Understanding and Guiding Young Female Athletes,</u> Caroline Selby and Shelly Smith say "children are supposed to play sports, not work sports." (p. 51) I agreed wholeheartedly. I just wanted her to have fun. I appreciated her entertaining ways and hoped she would never lose that spirit. I wanted her to dance barefoot in the tall grass. I wanted her to go on outings with kids in the neighborhood – play in the surf at the beach, chase butterflies and find happiness in a normal care-free childhood existence. "Here's the truth: You aren't a failure if you don't push your child to pursue every opportunity, and neither is your child. Your job is to cultivate your child's interests but to let her take the lead in pursuing them. When you feel the pressure to keep up with the Joneses, pull back and remind yourself that your child's path is unique." (Wiseman, p. 118)

Kimberly's path was indeed unique. It was unique in a way I hadn't imagined. Ironically, her path took us into the heart of where parents who push their children reside. It was a place where many parents forgot about the power of self-motivation. Yet, it was a place where self-motivation made a difference, especially among my daughter's age group.

According to Gesell and Ilg, self-motivation is the primary characteristic of the nine-year-old. She is able to summon reserves of energy and renew her attack for repeated trials at a difficult task. The nine-year-old is so interested in perfecting skills that she likes to do the same thing over and over again. She has greater interest in process and skill; she is more able to analyze her movements both before and during action. She seeks correction and explanation of her errors. She is more skillful in her motor performance and her timing is also under better control.

So my daughter pursued perfection while I wished for a more comfortable parenting experience. The expression "keeping up with the Joneses" became a private source of amusement. I wanted to keep up with the other Joneses –

people who tried not to be extraordinary, people who didn't push their children. I wanted to be around children who spent weekends with their families, not in serious training. We all need to remind ourselves that we are not our children's achievements, and external validation is not a reflection of our parenting skills. I needed to remind myself of these truths every day.

TOUGH LESSONS

*"....the threat of making her quit hit a nerve because she stopped crying
and focused on something besides winning."*

"She hates me!" Kimberly cried, as she got into the car for the long ride
home.

"Who hates you?" I asked, preparing myself for a talk about the importance
of getting along with the other girls.

"My coach!" she cried even louder, "and I hate her too!"

Wondering how I was going to deal with this new challenge, I bought some
time with a short response. "Well then, I guess that's, that," I replied. I
figured she needed time to cool down and, more importantly, I needed time
to think.

After a few minutes of sulking, she finally volunteered more information. "I
got in trouble because Rachel doesn't think I'm working hard enough, and
she said she's not going to let me compete on the bars."

The first meet was looming upon us and Kimi was struggling with her bar
routine. I still believed the problem was psychological. She simply didn't
depend on her arm, even though it was stronger than ever after the break. I
tried to explain to her that the coach didn't hate her; she pressured her
because she believed more effort meant improved skills. My words fell on
deaf ears.

So Kimi didn't compete on bars at the first meet, and that's all it took to get
her attention. She worked harder after that, although she still held back out
of fear. The struggle continued but, thankfully, her coach recognized the
change in attitude and identified the problem. One day, Kimi got into the
car after practice and declared, "You'll never guess what Rachel said to me

today."

Recognizing the positive tone in her voice, I was anxious to hear. I asked, "What did she say?"

"She said I can do it!" Kimi announced.

"Of course you can," I added, "but hearing your coach say it must make you feel good."

At the next meet, Kimberly competed on the bars and placed second. Rachel seemed amazed, and shared her astonishment with me. I gladly volunteered an explanation -her confidence made a strong impression. All my daughter needed was to hear the coach say, "you can do it." Expecting it might be a while before the coaching staff realized how much better my daughter performed in competition than she did during practice, I also told her that Kimi could rise to the occasion.

Months of hard work and well-deserved awards followed that first meet. Kimberly appeared on the podium at every meet, usually in the top five places. I expected her to be happy, but she became sullen. Anything less than first place simply wasn't her plan. We spent several car rides home with her in tears. It got frustrating for her father and me because we wanted her to be satisfied with her best performance. We wanted her to learn how to improve rather than constantly compare herself to others. We hoped she would learn an inward focus, take that focus to the gym, and develop a better work ethic.

On one torturous ride home following a second place award, I became fed up with her constant dissatisfaction. "You don't know how lucky you are," I declared angrily. "There are so many girls competing and only one who scored higher than you. Think about all the girls who didn't even get a medal. How do you think they feel? I bet they would love to have yours."

"But I want to WIN!" she exclaimed.

"We know you do, and sometimes you do win. You just can't win all the time. You are doing your best, and that should be good enough. You have to learn to be satisfied with doing your best. This is supposed to be fun. We take the whole day to drive you all over so you can compete. If you're not having fun, then you should quit."

"Never," she retorted.

"Then quit complaining, and try to have fun," I said.

"Be happy with what you got," Gregg chimed in.

I think the threat of making Kimi quit hit a nerve because she stopped crying and focused on something besides winning. It came as a relief to hear less complaining. She seemed happier to collect medals, regardless of the place. We all enjoyed a memorable year, and my daughter naturally improved.

At the State Championships, each gym was asked to enter a mini-team of four girls ages nine and under. The coaches selected Kimberly and three of her work-out buddies to compete. The experience gave my daughter a sense of accomplishment and belonging. I think she enjoyed that meet more than any other, and especially loved the camaraderie that she shared with her teammates.

On a personal level, Kimberly finished the season as the all-around 11th place gymnast for her age and level in the state of California. An even greater accomplishment was her 5th place standing on bars – something the coach gave great accolades for after such a rough start. She seemed content.

Kimberly also seemed to stop worrying excessively about what she perceived to be her placement in the gym. She competed with several other girls who were also her friends. They spent time together out of the gym: going to the movies, swimming, doing arts and crafts, and spending the night at each others houses. When some of these girls began moving to other groups for their workouts, Kimberly wanted to move "up" with them.

The group they were being moved to held more prestige for some reason and, naturally, she wanted to be a part of it.

Thankfully, instead of complaining, she worked harder. She pushed herself and asked the coaches what skills she needed in order to be moved. She also requested private lessons, which I hated to concede to. I thought she spent enough time in the gym. She pointed out to me that most of the girls she was trying to catch up to were getting private lessons. Once again, I felt trapped and, with great reluctance, I sucked it up. I wrote the checks and chauffeured her back and forth some more.

Our collective effort paid off. The day soon arrived when she received the news that she would be moving to the next group. She beamed with pride, and even dubbed the leotard she'd been wearing her "lucky Leo." For as long as it fit, she wore that black spaghetti strap with the pink and silver bubbles on it. As soon it was clean, it was on her little body. When it wasn't clean, she'd beg me to wash it, or wash it herself. I don't know if it was her new attitude or the lucky leotard, but that year turned out to be one of the most satisfying for me. It was on to the next competitive level, or so we thought.

To our surprise, and to Kimi's great disappointment, the coaching staff wanted her to compete at the same level for another year. We discussed it amongst ourselves and with the coaches. Our feeling was that she had performed well and accomplished quite a bit for a little girl who'd recently struggled to recover from a serious injury. We also felt that, in spite of her fun-loving approach to working out, she always rose to the occasion in competition. She was a fierce competitor. The coaching staff agreed, but felt that she needed to learn an important lesson about work ethic. She needed to focus on the details of her routines, not the power of her skills. She'd always been strong and flexible, able to master the skills to perfection. In competition, it was the minor deductions that adversely affected her scores. In the end, they left the decision up to us. She could move ahead if we wanted her to. We didn't know what to do. My gut reaction was to move her ahead. Once again, I thought the sport too serious for children. I also wondered whether all highly competitive gyms worked this way.

WHEN TO MEET WITH THE COACH
When you want to find out goals and a game plan for the near future (be sure to let the coach know this is your purpose and that you want to support him/her in communicating with your child)
When you want to discuss your role
When you want to know what is expected of your child
When you need information about the risks, rules, regulations or procedures of the sport
When you want to share positive feedback and/or concerns
When you want an understanding of certain decisions
When you want to negotiate or come to terms with expectations that you see as unreasonable or unclear

(Selby and Smith, pp. 70-71)

FIVE STEPS TO USE IN COACH - PARENT MEETINGS
Start with what is going well
Stick to a discussion about the child's behavior or performance that is of concern
Remember to avoid telling the coach what to do
Describe what you think your child needs
Suggest a plan that includes your own role in helping

(Selby and Smith, p. 71)

Coincidentally, Gregg's job situation seemed precarious at that time. His company experienced financial difficulties and had to issue lay-offs. He feared for his future and we considered relocation. My mother lived in Las Vegas, a booming economy at the time. It also happened to be the home town of Tasha Swikert, current World Champion gymnast. We decided to visit Mom – and Tasha's gym.

Before taking the trek to Las Vegas, I contacted the gym owner via e-mail and asked if Kimberly could work out with them for the week. She agreed. The visit introduced me to variations in gym philosophy. Our gym required every girl to compete as an all-around gymnast, meaning every athlete competed on every event. The Las Vegas gym encouraged athletes to progress differently. They allowed girls to compete at a higher level if they qualified on two events. If an individual girl wanted to compete for an all-around title, she decided for herself to compete at the lower level.

I also noticed a stark difference in the parent culture. Our gym had a parent viewing room with limited seating. The Las Vegas gym had a viewing room, but it was empty. No meddling, gossiping gym moms occupying the seats. I found it refreshingly different from what I'd been exposed to – appealing.

Sadly, Kimberly disagreed. She didn't like the differences, and she couldn't perform in a relaxed environment. She thrived on competition, even during practice. She wanted to be at a gym where coaches and athletes pushed harder. On the third day of our visit, she explained her preference to me.

"Everyone is too nice here, Mom." she said.

"What's wrong with being nice?" I inquired.

"Nothing. I'm just not used to it. It makes me uncomfortable," she replied.

"Tasha seems to like it, and she's a World Champion," I retorted.

"That's another thing. Even Tasha is sweet to me. The higher level girls at my gym hardly speak to us. I don't get it," she pondered.

"Well, every gym is different I guess," I said.

"I like mine better," she volunteered.

In addition to my daughter's self-realization, the job opportunities didn't pan out for Gregg, and I wasn't overly impressed with housing options. The idea of making such a huge move overwhelmed us all. I sucked it up and we returned home to make a decision about the next season.

After much consideration, discussion with Kimi, and prayer, we decided to have her compete at the same level for another year. It was a terrible blow to her self-esteem, especially since she saw girls who scored lower moving ahead. Whether she would use this as an opportunity to excel remained to be seen. Our little girl had a big lesson to learn, and I honestly didn't know at that point how strong her spirit was.

RESEARCH AND REFLECTION

I think of this year as "the year of almost." Kimberly was almost satisfied with her accomplishments and she almost made it to the top ten. We almost moved to a different State, almost promoted her to the next level, and I was almost successful at keeping my emotions in check. In short, it was a frustrating year for us all. And we almost didn't allow her to experience that frustration. We instinctively knew that protecting her from frustration or failure by demanding promotion was not in her best interest. It was better for her personal growth to stand by and watch her experience frustration, no matter how difficult. (Wisman)

I felt especially frustrated by my failed attempt to encourage Kimi. I knew my job as her mother. I understood the parent's roll. "…. When it's all over – whether she won or lost, performed perfectly or stumbled – praise her …. Fill her with messages of how proud you are of her talents, her courage, her gustiness." (Gadeberg, pp. 84-85) Yet, like all mothers sometimes do, I fell short in my parenting skills. I tried hard that year to deliver positive messages, knowing that my words fell on deaf ears.

I also let my parenting skills slip on occasion that year. The day that she cried because she thought her coach hated her is one example. Instead of pressuring her to work harder, I should have offered encouragement. According to Selby and Smith, guided discussions about the mental aspects of performance should focus on the positive; let her be the expert. If I had it to do over, I would have asked Kimberly what she thought about how hard she was working. I would have assured her that she would do well because that is what she wanted. In retrospect, my advise probably mattered little. She seemed to care most about the coach's opinion. When I tried to counsel her, it always fell on deaf ears.

The coach's confidence in Kimberly turned out to be the most important factor in her development that year. My daughter's performance improved as soon as she knew that Rachel cared about her. "Amanda Borden, 1996 Olympic gold medalist in gymnastics, attributed much of her success to her coach, Mary Lee Tracy. Factors she listed as important included feeling that her coach was her best friend: that her coach cared about her as a person first, and a gymnast second." (Selby and Smith, p. 54) Rachel made my daughter believe she cared about her as a person when she said, "You can do it." Rachel was a good coach.

I felt thankful for a good coach and Kimberly's development as an athlete. Yet, it worried me that she suddenly failed to be completely motivated by internal factors. I understood from educational research that it is normal for children to be motivated both extrinsically and intrinsically; however, this was a new and shocking characteristic for my daughter. In all her years, Kimi had been fiercely independent, self-reliant and dismissive about what other people thought. She concerned herself only with whatever it was that drove her – internally. I wondered what might be at the root of her personality change.

QUALITIES OF A GOOD COACH
Sets clear expectations
Chooses athletes based on merit
Gives everyone equal opportunity
Never abuses athletes – physically or verbally
Disciplines by making athletes work harder
Holds athletes accountable
Doesn't allow parents to make excuses
Doesn't demean the opposition
Keeps head cool in the face of irate parents
Tells athletes "Do your best and I will be proud"

QUALITIES IN A BAD COACH
Plays favorites
Knows and protects his/her power, even at the expense of children's welfare
Withholds praise, gives the cold shoulder to control athletes
Values winning more than good sportsmanship
Demeans athletes
Punishes under-performance or disloyalty with abuse

THINGS TO LOOK FOR IN COACHING
Healthy environment
Adaptation to individual needs (i.e., response to motivators – negative vs. positive)
Values that match your own (i.e., how important is winning?)
Someone who includes athlete input in decision-making and adjusts goals and game plans accordingly, providing technical expertise and support along the way

(Selby and Smith)

I wondered if the change in Kimberly's personality meant her self-esteem was in jeopardy. I started paying closer attention. And I researched self-esteem among athletes. "One study found that female gymnasts who trained in environments they perceived to be task oriented – those that rewarded hard work and personal improvement and promoted cooperative learning – had higher self-esteem, better body images, less stress, and more enjoyment of their sport than did those athletes who trained in environments they perceived to be ego oriented – those that encouraged rivalry among athletes and winning at all costs and in which greater attention was paid to the most talented athletes." (Selby and Smith, p. 53). Kimi's gym environment rewarded hard work and personal improvement. It also encouraged rivalry among athletes. It had to. All individual sports, by definition, promote rivalry. The way around this problem is to focus on cooperative learning and treat less talented athletes the same as those who show promise. Cooperative learning is easy to facilitate. Equal treatment of unequal talent is not an easy task. And Kimi's gym shared the challenge of dealing with unequal talent.

Kimberly's gym was also not immune to problems that affect female athletes' self-esteem, including eating disorders. Rumors of an older girl with an eating disorder spread through the gym community, and it frightened me. Eating disorders plague female athletes who are in sports emphasizing smallness, thinness or low weight. Eating disorders especially plague girls in sports where the athlete is likely to display her body in a form fitting leotard or swimsuit. Furthermore, many sports psychologists believe there is a strong correlation between a high achieving athlete and an addictive-compulsive personality type: perfectionism, willingness to please, willingness to move through pain, and a high desire to comply with the expectation of others. (Zimmerman) Kimberly was in a sport emphasizing smallness, she wore a leotard, and she had a high achieving personality. Her recent eagerness to please gave me cause for concern. The last thing I wanted to do was set my daughter up for psychological problems. I knew I had to be diligent about caring for her diet, making sure she felt secure, and giving her a sense of control.

THE CHAMPIONSHIP
Of course I felt proud. What mother wouldn't?

"Are you sure we made the right decision?" I asked Rachel. We'd been to several competitions and Kimi won almost every event without a struggle.

"Why?" she replied.

"Well, it looks like winning is coming a little too easy for Kimi, and it doesn't seem fair to the other girls."

"Aren't you glad she's winning?" she asked.

"Sure," I responded, "I'm happy for her."

"Then don't worry about the other girls. Stand up and shout 'That's my girl!' That's what the other mom's would do in your place," she added. "Besides, the toughest competition is yet to come."

Sadly, I could never see myself standing and shouting, "That's my girl!" Another reminder of how I didn't fit in.

During the following weeks, Kimberly continued to collect medals. On one hand, I was happy for her. She was finally getting the first place medals that she yearned for. It seemed to do wonders for her self-esteem and helped her develop a stronger affinity for the gym. Her bond with the coaching staff and the other girls strengthened as she blossomed with success. On the other hand, I feared the season wouldn't provide a learning opportunity. I feared she wouldn't develop a better work ethic, as I'd hoped. I desperately tried to suppress my desire for her to excel in a less ostentatious manner. I reminded myself daily that this was, perhaps, a once-in-a-lifetime opportunity, and the confidence she was building made it all worthwhile.

Admittedly, I shared some of her pride. Of course I did. What mother wouldn't feel proud? She was a valuable team member, a role model for lower level girls, and my glowing offspring. At every meet, the coaches used her scores in the team totals and, at every meet, the team won first place. In and out of the gym, my daughter's latest scores became a topic of conversation. In the gym and in the bleachers, younger girls watched her with adoring eyes and sought out opportunities to interact with her. During work-outs, Kimi became a standard of excellence. At competitions, she was the one to watch. She was happy, and that made life enjoyable.

Yet, I felt bad for the other girls – girls who'd been working a lot harder than my daughter. I felt worse for some of their moms – mothers who appeared to invest more than I did in this sport. Facing them after a competition was often difficult, and I vacillated between feeling guilty and amused. I tried to figure out a comfortable protocol, but never could. All I ever thought about was the fastest way to the door.

At the gym, other mothers suddenly asked for my opinion and advice. I tried to offered good advice, but felt ill at ease. After all, I faced insurmountable challenges as a gym mom. I reluctantly resided in a world that ran contrary to my instincts. I thought my daughter had an unhealthy perspective, I didn't truly believe in her sport, I was unsuccessful at providing other outlets, and I could not discuss other options for her. In a different world, I would have been able to share recommendations for the sisterhood of gym moms (see chart on following page).

My concern for Kimi's effortless winning soon came to an end. Rachel warned her about the dangers of getting too comfortable. Challengers want to beat the girl on top of the podium. Everyone knows that. Well, almost everyone knows that. When it comes to little girls, I'm not sure the girl on the podium is developmentally capable of understanding this truth. The girls who wanted to beat Kimberly's scores were very aware, and so were their mothers. They demonstrated a sense of determination and work ethic that I still hoped my daughter would develop. The mothers encouraged their sense of determination, and the number of private lessons increased as the season progressed.

RECOMMENDATIONS FOR THE SISTERHOOD OF GYM MOMS (AND OTHERS)
Share examples of successful female athletes, especially gymnasts
Maintain a healthy perspective of what your daughter is capable of doing at her age – be realistic about what she can and cannot do
Leave room for your daughter's personality because every girl is unique
Avoid the trap of living vicariously through her – get a life!
Believe in her. Truly
Be involved but not overly involved – get a life!
Frame and display examples of her in action, but keep them to yourself please
Encourage mixed gender social groups – let her have a life outside this gym
Emphasize enjoyment rather than competition
Discuss various scenarios for your daughter's future
Avoid an emphasis on appearance and/or weight (coaches' comments, weigh-ins, body fat testing, dietary controls or meal planning, and any other message that tells a girl there's some relationship between body fat and performance)

Kimi's work-out buddy had a solid work ethic and a strong sense of determination, and she improved dramatically. By the end of the season, the two girls alternated first place medals. At the Sectional Meet for competitors from Southern California, Kimberly finished second place in the all-around championship. Her gym buddy won the first place award. For the first time, my daughter truly understood the notion of work ethic. She realized that she should have been taking her coach's warnings more seriously.

With the state meet looming, my Kimi decided to increase her effort. She asked for private lessons and told Rachel that she wanted to win. The wise coach told my daughter that she had her work cut out for her. Believing it, Kimberly worked harder than ever before. It was clear to me that she had the determination of a winner. She prepared faithfully and waited patiently. Finally, I thought, my daughter's developed a work ethic.

The night before the State meet, we drove north to Santa Barbara. We usually stayed in the same hotel with other families from the team and this meet was no different. I never really understood the point of that exercise since bedtime came early in preparation for the next day. I remember thinking it odd that they considered it time spent together. Rarely did the team even eat breakfast together. The girls shared scarce moments to horse around before bedtime. Those few moments provided a sense of team spirit and goodwill. In reality, it was often their own teammates that the girls competed against. They needed goodwill.

Kimberly felt painfully aware that she had to compete against her teammate at the State Championship that year. They were workout buddies, but they also pushed each other to excel. They challenged each other at practice and at every meet. They both wanted to win, but only one could. My daughter understood this and demonstrated a fresh determination to achieve her goal.

My daughter's sense of determination at the meet seemed extraordinary. Her confidence could not be shaken, and her performance dazzling. She finished first place on every event except beam – ironically her best event. Yes! She accomplished her goal, becoming the all-around State Champion. She beamed like a Christmas tree for weeks after that. Of course I did, too. I shared her happiness and gladly assumed the role of proud mama.

A few weeks later, Kimberly's team traveled to the State Team meet. I think of that day as the highlight of my daughter's gymnastics experience. She traveled with five teammates to compete against other teams from across California. The girls felt like family after the number of hours they spent in preparation. They shared a true sense of belonging, and they were excited to be working together instead of competing against one another.

The girls' hard work that year culminated in an unprecedented win. Their combined scores found no match on any apparatus. For the first time in the history of her gym, the team won on every event. Their picture was in the paper, and the girls shared a strong camaraderie. Kimberly's favorite coach, Rachel, was voted coach of the year by the gymnastics association. Gymnasts, parents and coaches all shared in the excitement.

Kimi's hard work that year also gave our family a sense of satisfaction. As a result of her effort, my daughter accomplished the goal of winning. She broke a record on the floor event, scoring a 9.75. She also won the highly coveted "Most Valuable" award. To this day, she appreciates that award the most. It serves as a reminder of the rare team opportunities in gymnastics. Being part of a team taught Kimberly greater appreciation for friendship and cooperative efforts. For that lesson, I am particularly grateful. I strongly value friendships, and my daughter still maintains relationships with some of her gym buddies. The team competition also gave Kimi an early life experience at working well with others – a skill that should benefit her in future work environments.

RESEARCH AND REFLECTION

Outwardly I supported my daughter and her gym. For the reasons I've already stated in this chapter, I appreciate the benefits realized by our experience. However, internally, I continued to carry on a conversation with myself about the decisions we made. I continued to rationalize our choice, because the reality of the experience challenged my desire for an uncomplicated life.

The world of competitive gymnastics is so very unique. It is a brutally intense sport, demanding intense commitment from children under the age of 18. The workouts are exhilarating and grueling all at the same time, lasting three to four hours a day. Competitors train four to six days a week, year round. Such commitment is unmatched by almost all other sports. Skills are accomplished incrementally so there is always a new challenge ahead. Coaches, and sometimes parents, are extremely tough on the athletes. However, athletes are often toughest on themselves, harder than coaches, parents and the competition. It was complicated.

Coaches often micro-manage in order to get results. That is not to say that there are countless gyms whose coaches do not micro manage their talent. Many gym training philosophies focus on fun rather than winning. To produce winning athletes, however, coaches have to focus on the minute details of routines and training, for that is the basis of their scores. They insist on regular attendance, allow little or no rest periods during the three to four hour work outs each day, and reward those who consistently perform well. It is no surprise that athletes who comply with a high coaching standard usually spend more time on the podium than their competition.

Time on the podium is a gymnast's coveted reward, and my daughter was no exception. There is no such thing as professional gymnastics, so the highest achievement in gymnastics is an opportunity to compete in the Olympics. Injury and burnout rates are high, and every year competition gets tougher. The chance of representing gymnastics to the world is slim. If you are unfamiliar with the sport, I'm sure it all sounds unrewarding. You may even wonder what draws so many families to the sport. To be precise, there are over 4,000 clubs nationwide offering gymnastics instruction to over three million young people. More than 91,500 of those young people are registered competitors. Kimberly somehow understood that the State Championship classified her as unique. And I knew this understanding strengthened her commitment to the sport.

At the ripe young age of ten, Kimberly worked harder with each passing day. Her time in the gym seemed endless with no sign of a slowing period. I feared my time with her would continue to diminish. She was a little girl whose childhood was slipping away, and I longed for the time we didn't have together. I worried whether the number of hours she spent in the gym might have an adverse affect on her development. According to Payne and Issacs, weight bearing activities stimulate increased bone density. But they also say that "more stimulation is not always better" when it comes to programs designed to enhance early motor development. (p. 101). So which is it? I knew by looking at gymnasts on television that growth must be affected by the sport. Once again, I considered taking my daughter and running from the gym life.

Yet Kimberly was happier than she'd ever been. How could I seriously think about denying her that joy? She accomplished her goal, won more time on the podium than the previous year, and saw nothing but blue skies in the horizon. I saw the calm satisfaction written all over her face. According to Gurian (2002), cognitive development is complete by ten years of age. Ten is relaxed and casual, yet alert. She has herself and her skills in hand; she takes things in stride; she works with executive speed and likes the challenge ... It is said that the ten-year-old sometimes values her peer group more than her family. Kimberly definitely had her skills in hand and held her gym buddies in high regard.

It was the longing for my daughter that brought me to a new crossroad. I needed a different sort of relationship with her – one that focused on life outside of gymnastics. We tried to make time on the weekends for social outings, but between family commitments and competition, it seemed impossible. Her social group at school was limited due to the number of hours she she spent training. And Kimi started asking to be home-schooled because some of her gym buddies were home-schooled. They spent more time at the gym than girls in public school, and that's what she wanted. For selfish reasons, I favored the idea. We discussed it, talked with other parents, and I researched the methodology. Then we spent a few months thinking it over. Excited about the final decision to begin home-schooling, I anticipated a closer relationship with my little girl.

WHOSE DREAM IS IT, ANYWAY?

I hated myself.....

"What are those girls doing, Mom?" Kimberly asked me one day as we arrived at the gym for a private lesson. About half-a-dozen girls in Kimi's age group appeared to be in some sort of group lesson. Two of the moms I'd been friendly with were sitting in the viewing room, and one of them piped in with an explanation.

"They just started a special group today," she said. "It's called TOPS. They will do the training but they are not going to compete with other TOPS groups."

I'd never heard of TOPS, but as I looked at the members of the group, it was obvious that they'd picked top performers. Puzzled, I looked over at my daughter, who made the same observation.

"How come I'm not invited?" Kimi asked.

The disappointment in her voice pulled at my heart strings, and seeing that group of girls took me by surprise. The coaches assembled their youngest talent without notifying the booster club. It didn't give the rest of us a chance to learn about the group's purpose. It didn't give us time to discover criteria for participation. It didn't give us time to adjust and prepare our daughters. It didn't give me an opportunity to develop a plan before coming upon the group by accident. Feeling shocked and unprepared to support my daughter through the disappointment left me powerless. I let my emotions run away with me, and lost my temper.

"It's a "special group," so I guess this is just for "special" girls," I said sarcastically, and stormed out the door.

One of the other mothers followed me outside. I was so upset that I didn't even know how to respond to her approach. In that instant, I was tired of being nice. She apologized for not calling to tell me about TOPS, but said she had been sworn to secrecy. My blood pressure elevated, and I became offensive. I told her to worry about her own daughter. And then it hit me: I was one of them – a gym mom! My behavior caused immediate feelings of regret and self doubt. I wanted to run and hide. If I didn't apologize, I should have.

I became self absorbed for weeks after that incident. I wanted to crawl out of my own skin. I hated myself. In spite of my best effort, I found myself overly involved in Kimberly's sport. The thought of becoming overly involved disgusted me. My attitude needed serious adjustment, and I knew it. I spent the week contemplating my own interest in Kimberly's passion. I vented. I cried. I prayed. I vented some more, cried some more and prayed earnestly.

I knew the importance of learning to function in the gym. The longer my daughter remained a gymnast, the stronger my realization became. Her activity required parent participation. The sport, by definition attracts girls and parents who are driven to achieve. Sacrifices are encouraged, sometimes required, and many parents honestly believe their parenting skills are measured by their children's athletic performance. "This aggressiveness can result in destructive behavior that includes pushing the girls too far, allowing un-sportsmanlike conduct, and worse." (Wiseman) I feared the bad behavior would soon spread to the girls. So far, my daughter and her work-out buddies had little or no conflict. All of the bad behavior I witnessed up to that point came from the parents. The girls were still young, but approaching an age where, in the best of circumstances they would grow testy. I had to suck it up and learn new social skills, for Kimi's sake.

Of course this period of introspection and learning couldn't be conducted in a vacuum. Kimberly, still in the lurch, wondered why she hadn't been invited to join the new group. We heard more about TOPS every day, and the more my daughter heard, the stronger her desire grew. She wanted to be a member of that special group. She wanted to be with the girls she usually worked out with, and she complained daily. I could only think of one solution and suggested that she ask her coach if she could join the group.

At the same time, I called the owner of the gym. I wanted to ask why the management failed to notify parents about the new group, but decided against it for various reasons. First, I believed questioning management could not affect change. More importantly, I feared such questioning might be social suicide, and I had just committed to learning new social skills in the gym environment.

REASONS WHY PEOPLE DON'T CONFRONT LEGITIMATE ISSUES
Fear that they will be unable to affect change
Knowledge that others have tried and failed
Fear of making things worse
Fear of social suicide
Thinking that the issue may not be that big a deal
Belief that the issue may be outside ones purview
Turning the other cheek (martyrdom)
Belief that it's "stooping" to a lower level

I restricted my inquiry to matters that affected my daughter rather than the gym at large. I asked about the group's purpose and the criteria for joining it. I asked about Kimberly's chances of being included. For my daughter's sake, I argued on her behalf. I told the owner that Kimberly would benefit from TOPS training because the group was small, the coaching staff was more advanced than her regular coaches, and the girls were focused. I also reminded her that Kimi performed well in competition, and her scores directly benefited the gym.

The owner explained that the coaches selected only home-schooled girls because they trained in the morning. She also confirmed that they were selected based on their potential. They intended to fast track a small group of girls who showed the potential of becoming elite gymnasts. The owner agreed with my reasons for including Kimi in the group but was unaware that we home-schooled. She then questioned my daughter's work ethic, saying it might adversely affect her potential. It always boiled down to that.

After the phone call, I told Kimi that if she really wanted to be in the TOPS group she had to, once again, stop playing around and work harder in the gym. I also reminded her of my advice to ask if she could join the group. She heeded that advice and made her request the following day. I'm sure the coaches saw it coming, and told her it was only for girls who worked hard. The saying "What have you done for me lately?" comes to mind. Sure she was the most valuable team member and broke records, but that was last season.

Rachel told Kimi to "get with the program," so, my daughter spent the next few weeks proving that she was serious. Her work ethic improved, but it didn't come easy. She enjoyed playing at the gym and failed to understand the importance of working harder when she could win as easily as she did. Once again, she was forced to "suck it up" and deal with an uncomfortable situation. Every day she worked hard, and every day she asked her coach, "Did I work hard enough today?"

Finally, after what seemed like forever to Kimberly, the coaches allowed her to join the group she had so longed for. She glowed with contentment, and everybody seemed genuinely happy for her. Several of the other mothers made comments like "it's about time!" I felt relief – happy for my daughter. I also felt a little proud, and shared her recent success with almost anyone who would listen.

After three years and a State Championship, it seemed impossible to get away from the topic of gymnastics. By that time, everyone in our social network knew about Kimi's accomplishments and wondered about her future in gymnastics. Anyone who knew her understood her passion. Even when I made a point to engage in activities outside of the gym, I found myself conversing on the subject. In spite of my best efforts, I spent a good portion of my time in her world, and I knew that I'd have to accept that reality as long as she trained. Because she was a child, the world of gymnastics couldn't be hers and hers alone – her parents had to be involved. I had to be involved. Our worlds were enmeshed and, by default, her goals became our goals. I confess. I got caught up in it. I think it was my mother who asked, "Whose dream is it anyway?"

I reflected on that little girl who'd drawn pictures of herself on the podium at the Olympics. I realized my excitement was a reflection of Kimi's belief that the dream could become reality. And I knew I lost myself somewhere along the way. I knew I had to make the journey back to myself or be in danger of permanent transition to gym-motherhood. I never wanted to use my daughter for self-gratification, so I had to remember my own ambitions. I had to remind myself that I had a life separate from hers. I needed more activities outside the gym.

I believed I must stay grounded for another important reason. The best tools of parenting include wisdom and maturity. Children need parental wisdom to guide them through the challenges of life. Parents need maturity to negotiate those challenges successfully. The odds of a gymnast becoming an Olympian are slim. At this phase, my reality and her reality were developmentally opposite. She would need a mature perspective when the time came for her to deal in the adult world. I knew the future held certain disappointment, and I knew Kimberly would need me to help her through it. For now, though, she was just a child. She did not understand statistical realities. For now, she only required my support.

RESEARCH AND REFLECTION

While Kimberly struggled for membership in an elite group, I supported and guided her. In reality, I feared the prospect of joining that group. I quietly wondered what was so fun about her sport. The inception of TOPS at our gym brought out the worst in parents. It served to encourage competition among us. After all, the group was special, and it included only the best athletes. Some of the other mothers behaved as if it were their life's ambition for their daughters to go to the Olympics. And I thought, "Really? We're talking about prepubescent children!" In the words of the experts, "When the Olympics starts to become more of a goal for (the mother) than for her daughter...(the mother) would need to take a long look at her commitment and motives." (Selby and Smith, p. 91) I found no enjoyment in a place where women live vicariously through their daughters. And there was more...

Watching other mothers behave badly came easily, but facing my own misconduct came with great pain. Apparently, parents often fail to recognize their own misconduct in childhood sports. According to Wiseman, parents are good at assuming the worst about everyone else but are not good at recognizing their own wrongdoing. If only I could have ignored my own misconduct. I saw myself behaving badly, yet I had no idea how to avoid it. As a parent, I simply failed to control my emotions. As a defense mechanism, I decided to become even more knowledgeable about gymnastics. Knowledge is power, right?

I began reading more and watching gymnastics on television. About that time, one of the television networks ran a special on TOPS. The documentary disturbed me, and I came away from it feeling relieved that our gym didn't participate in the national competition. The film depicted coaches and parents pushing very small children beyond their capacity. Coaches yelled and worked the girls too hard. Parents, especially mothers, went to great lengths to be sure their daughters qualified. One small girl was forced to compete injured. Her mother told her to "suck it up." I was appalled. What possible benefit could a parent realize through such compulsory behavior? Why do we care if a small child qualifies for a special group? Will it matter in ten years? I answered my own questions but couldn't feel completely satisfied. I experienced an odd confliction that left me paralyzed. Why did my daughter drive herself to be part of this world?

Once again, I sucked it up. However uncomfortable for me, Kimberly chose gymnastics and thrived in its environment. I knew she both needed and benefited from this world. Ours is a competitive culture, and a competitive culture encourages attitudes of superiority – by creating special groups. Competition also teaches work ethic and motivates children to do their best. "The evidence points to a simple fact: playing sports helps our daughters grow into healthy, strong women. As parents, as educators, as members of the human community, we need to recognize this fact. It carries with it a responsibility. We need to make athletics an integral part of our daughters' childhood, so that their ownership of it is something they take for granted, like air or sunlight. We need to stitch it into the fabric of their lives." (Zimmerman, p. 238) Well, Kimberly stitched gymnastics into the fabric of our lives regardless of my feelings on the matter.

Following my own outburst and introspection, I no longer blamed other parents for getting caught up in the culture of gymnastics. Today's social climate promotes intensive, often obsessive mothering. If gymnastics magnifies intensity and obsessive parenting, there is good reason. The precious, unique, individual girl in this sport gets the gold. It's every man, or woman, for himself. For most parents, it is narcissism centered on children (Douglas and Michaels 2004). It must be difficult for any mother to find balance between giving her daughter opportunities and using her for her own narcissistic purposes. And how can mothers distinguish between the two?

As I vacillated between wanting to belong and wanting to run away, I knew I had to take a critical look at my concessions. I worried about whether my perspective was a self-righteous one. The other moms clearly fit into a social hierarchy. Was I incapable of seeing how I fit into the subculture to which I must have belonged? I continued to distance myself emotionally from the world of gymnastics lest it swallow me whole. Again, I promised myself more time away from the gym – focusing on some of my own interests.

I felt alone. Part of me longed to feel a sense of belonging without question. Part of me wanted to join the group wholeheartedly, maybe even run for office in the booster club. Yet, thinking rationally about those feelings, I considered them pathetic. I wanted to fight narcissism with everything in me. I wonder why both feelings, neither of them good, tortured my soul. Turning to an external source, I found words of wisdom: "Everyone wants to belong somewhere. There's nothing weak or pathetic about it – it's a universal drive. It's just that our true character is revealed in the moments when that belonging comes at the cost of what we believe in and what we know is right." (Wiseman, p. 25) I suppose that sums it up.

AGONY

I found myself choking back tears....

"Hello, Lora?"

It was one of the coaches on the phone. Having been through it once already, I knew she wasn't calling to tell me about Kimberly's latest tumbling pass. My heart sank.

"What's wrong?" I blurted.

"Um.... yeah, it's her leg. She broke it vaulting. I'm sure it's broken. She's icing it right now. Do you want us to call an ambulance, or are you close?"

"We're just down the street. We'll be right there."

Gregg and I left our dinner where it sat and rushed to the gym. We couldn't get there fast enough. The five minute trip seemed like an hour, and as we pulled into the parking lot, parents pointed us to the back of the gym, near the vault mats. A few worried people surrounded my daughter, her best friend in tears. Most of the gymnasts remained at their work-out stations but stared in her direction. Kimberly sat propped up on a mat icing her leg. She wore a crooked grin.

As I approached, she seemed shocked. When I got to her side, she explained that she over-rotated and landed "funny." She said she heard it snap. With that piece of information, I felt the blood drain from my face and sat down next to her trying to be strong. She was stronger. She looked at me as if to say, "Suck it up, Mom. I'm fine. I'm good – just a scratch .... Be back in no time."

Gregg and one of the coaches carried Kimberly to the car, being careful not to jar her leg on the way. We drove her straight to the hospital, with her moaning at every turn. By the time we arrived at the hospital parking lot, she writhed in pain, and expected to receive immediate attention. My daughter's patience wore thin by the time we entered the building. She began to request medicine in a rather loud voice. But she never shed a tear.

When the hospital staff found a bed for Kimberly and lifted the ice bag, I noticed bone bulging just above her ankle. I found myself choking back the tears that my daughter refused to shed. Thankfully, a doctor who recognized her from the gym soon approached, preventing my certain break-down. The head surgical nurse, who also knew her from the gym, accompanied him. As the medical staff consulted with Gregg, my baby was wheeled off to radiology. Isolated and in shock, I took those few moments to let my emotions out, then collect myself.

"I can't do this anymore," I cried to Gregg when we finally got a minute to ourselves. "What are we doing?" He, being the wise one in such matters, knew how to console me and save the discussion for later. He hugged me, let me cry, and handed me a box of tissues. I knew I was being placated, but I also knew there was nothing more to be done. I suppressed my rage and waited for the medical decision.

Kimberly needed immediate surgery to repair breaks to her fibula and tibia – compound fractures to both bones in her lower leg. They wheeled her off and we waited. Three agonizing hours later, we met her in recovery and prepared for a night in the hospital. Thank God for that over-night stay! A broken fib-tib is, apparently, one of the most painful breaks. Even though she never cried, my daughter did experience pain. She expresses her pain through anger, and that night she seemed particularly angry. I'm sure she doesn't remember because of the medication, but she had the disposition of a rattlesnake. I requested additional morphine equaling twice the prescribed amount to get her through the night.

I remember that night as physically painful for Kimberly and heart-wrenching for me. However, the recovery period that followed made that night seem easy. The following three to four months were a living hell. My daughter had three pins in her leg, requiring three stages of recovery. She remained in a cast for weeks while the pins helped keep her bones in place. Once the bones solidified, she went in for pin removal. Removing the pins turned out to be an excruciating experience for both of us. The blood drained from my face as I witnessed her endurance. I felt nausea as she became angry, and I feared she might start screaming four-letter explicatives. She sucked it up and moved on to the second stage of recovery – another cast.

We learned to live with our daughter, the invalid. Or should I say we did our best at learning to live with her as an invalid? Everywhere we went, the crutches went. Everywhere we wanted to go, we had to rethink because most of our normal routine involved physical activity. With the exception of a summer vacation at the beach that we had already scheduled, life changed dramatically.

The dramatic change was punctuated by Kimi's moods. For a while she continued going to the gym for strength training and demonstrated her ability to "suck it up." Wanting to prove she was able to work through the temporary disability, she shocked the coaches by doing press-ups with her leg in a cast. She also continued going to TOPS for conditioning and training. It was intense, but she worked out with that group to the best of her ability –until frustration got the better of her.

Kimberly hated being incapacitated and, eventually, she let disappointment wear her down. She responded by showing everyone around her just how sour her disposition could become. Nothing seemed to please her, and everyone knew exactly how displeased the condition made her feel. She longed to be in training and complained regularly. When she wasn't complaining, she displayed outbursts of anger. We chastised her almost daily and, in time, her anger turned to apathy.

Kimi started spending a good part of gym time in the team room playing cards with a group of girls who also felt less than capable of a full work-out. The group commiserated over their respective injuries and provided support for one another. A forgotten group, they huddled together in a room filled with varying degrees of apathy, waiting for the day when they could return to practice. Most of the girls had sprains, headaches or stomach ailments.

An older girl, who'd also broken her leg, befriended my daughter in spite of their age difference. They shared the same surgeon and physical therapist, giving them greater commonality. They supported each other through the weary stages of recovery. As I studied them attending gym regularly, in spite of their incapacitation, I wondered why. Why did they have to be there? In the face of minimal work-outs, I didn't understand how being at the gym could either enhance their recovery or improve their attitude. Both girls seemed jaded.

Kimberly became increasingly worn down by rehabilitation and ever more discouraged at watching her teammates work out without her. By the time she reached the final stage of rehabilitation, she seemed less enamored with the gym. Physical therapy came to be the highlight of her day. The therapists gave her special attention – attention that she missed receiving from her coaches and teammates. Their attention, combined with the new bonds she'd made among other injured gymnasts, created a sense of disenfranchisement.

Kimberly's focus changed during rehabilitation. Before we knew what happened, she announced to the coaches that she was dropping out of TOPS –the special group that she had worked so hard to join. Physical injury took its toll, more mentally than physically. We didn't know how to help her recover. The upcoming season and a renewed thrill of competition gave us hope. But secretly, I hoped we were approaching the end of our gymnastics years.

RESEARCH AND REFLECTION

My worst fear came true. Kimberly was injured again. I again questioned her involvement in gymnastics. I tired of the injuries, the physical therapy, and the disappointments. I felt particularly fed up with the overall culture of the sport. Gymnasts suffer injury and dedicate their lives to the gym. That's reality. But they are just children! Children don't belong in a culture that includes unnecessary physical injury. Children especially don't belong in a culture that makes light of those injuries. Wondering what the experts had to say, I conducted research.

According to Payne and Issacs, overuse injuries result from putting children's' muscular and skeletal systems under repeated stress over long periods of time. Overuse injuries are more prevalent as specialization becomes more important and workouts get longer. Overuse injuries should be taken seriously. If activity is not curtailed in this class of injury, permanent injury could result. Young gymnasts often continue to work out with overuse injuries such as Osgood-Schlatter's or Sever's disease. These are the two most prevalent injuries that result from overuse and inefficient stretching. (Payne and Issacs)

AMERICAN ACADEMY OF PEDIATRICS RECOMMENDATIONS FOR INURY PREVENTION
Proper conditioning
Avoidance of excess in training
Appropriate competitive environment
Complete resolution of a prior injury
Appropriate supervision
Rule changes
Instruction in correct bio-mechanics
Appropriate equipment
Complete pre-participation physical assessment
Appropriate matching of competitors

I recognized Kimberly's injury as a warning sign, but found myself paralyzed. I believed that quitting had to be her decision, not mine. I couldn't face the prospect of regret or resentment. If I forced her to quit because of my intuition, she might hate me for the rest of her life. Her passion for gymnastics created a perfect condition for remorse over losing it. She was too young to grieve. I had to suck it up and bide my time.

DEVASTATION

.... you could have heard a pin drop as the paramedics took my baby out on a stretcher.

Kimberly healed and the doctor released her for competition by mid-October. The coaches wanted her to move to the next level in the spring, but she had to compete at least once in the fall. The season had almost ended; in fact, all that remained were the Sectional and State Championships. To compete in Sectionals, a gymnast must qualify through previous meets during the season. We thought she'd lost her chance to move up in the spring, but the coaches surprised us by petitioning her into Sectionals. Apparently, the review board considers past performance, and her State Championship made a difference. She received the good news a week before the event.

It had been a year since her last meet, so Kimberly seemed particularly elated. Her greatest thrill came in competition. Saying she loved to compete is an understatement. My daughter lived to compete. She also wanted to demonstrate her ability to perform well after an injury. And she had a sense of certainty unlike any I had seen in her. It was as if she knew she could go to competition and perform well, in spite of the obstacles that stood in her path. I felt grateful to be over the recovery phase and happy to see her in her element once again. However, I felt less grateful about the prospect of returning to the bleachers.

I suffered most in the bleachers, and the suffering was bad enough to become a physical discomfort. Kimberly thrived on competition but I didn't – especially in this atmosphere. I hated supporting Kimberly's passion on competition days. Crowds, nervous parents, serious coaches, scowling judges, and dangerous activity put my stomach in knots. I tried hard to focus on fun rather than danger. I tried to sit with the calm parents rather than the quintessential "gym moms." I tried to ignore angry coaches and self-impressed judges. I refrained from retreat to the car. I often found

65

myself wandering in the background at the vending booths, reminding myself that Kimi lived for gymnastics. I sucked it up and put on a cheerful facade for her sake.

On the day of the Sectional meet, we proceeded to the gym and dropped Kimi off at the team entrance, then made our way to the stands. As we sat waiting for our daughter's first event, Gregg prepared the video camera. Many of the other parents acknowledged our presence and congratulated us on our daughter's return. The atmosphere around us seemed relatively calm as Kimi chalked up for her bar routine warm-ups. We continued idle chatter amongst ourselves while waiting nervously for the competition to begin.

Once the warm-ups ended, Kimberly stood at the bars for her routine to be judged. She saluted the judges and mounted beautifully. It appeared as if she had the form and grace of a champion. She took nice, high tap swings on the high bar –higher and tighter than I'd seen in practice. As usual, she intensified her performance for competition.

Then it happened. All of a sudden, my daughter flew off the bars, clawing in mid-air like a cat. As I saw her landing head first on the mat, all I could do was mutter, "Lord, no!" Gregg dropped the video camera and ran down the bleachers. I followed close behind.

While coaches and trainer loomed over our girl, we stood at the sidelines in shock. Not knowing if we could enter the competition zone, I waited and prayed. After what seemed like an eternity, the coach motioned us to join them. Kimberly smiled that crooked smile and insisted she was fine. She wanted to get up and finish her routine, of course, but the trainer refused to allow it. He said that her first attempt had been sketchy. He took her out of the competition and called an ambulance. Psychologically devastated by the unfortunate turn of events, Kimberly sat in shock.

Everyone in the gym sat in shock. You could have heard a pin drop as the paramedics took my baby out on a stretcher. "Our prayers are with you," people muttered as we followed her out the door. I barely remember the trip to the hospital, or the time we spent there. I only remember saying to myself, "I'm done with this. No more gymnastics." I felt overwhelmed by the stress of constantly "sucking it up." Gymnastics had taken over our lives, and not in a good way. All I could think about was manipulating her out of the sport without making her hate me. Believing Gregg would continue to support her passion, I could hardly discuss my thoughts with him.

As I sat brooding, a doctor appeared with preliminary results. The X-rays showed no broken bones, so he referred Kimberly to her primary care physician and sent her home. We had something to be grateful for. However, seeing Kimberly dive headfirst to the floor outweighed my feelings of gratitude. We endured a quiet ride home, and numerous fires in Southern California served to further blacken the day. I prayed for guidance. The answer to my prayers came when we visited her doctor the following week. He restricted her from training – period, and ordered her to stay out of the gym all together.

"For how long?" she asked, with a look of disbelief on her face. She'd never been exiled from the gym.

"I don't know," the doctor responded, "at least until the week before Thanksgiving. We have to be sure your neck is completely healed before you take any risks."

She sat in dissatisfied silence as I thanked the doctor for his time and gathered our belongings. Then we proceeded home and waited for the holiday. As expected, Kimberly's temperament became testy in the absence of her beloved sport. Patience never had been her strong suit and this time was no different than the rest. She sulked. She pouted. She isolated herself in her room. When she did come out, I found myself wishing she would return. Thanksgiving weekend didn't arrive quickly enough.

The State Championship was scheduled for Thanksgiving weekend, so once again, the coaches petitioned Kimberly to compete. When we received the news, her mood improved dramatically. She bubbled over in anticipation. However, her hopes quickly reduced to rubble. A week before the meet, the doctor sent her for an MRI. The results showed a severe injury to the ligamentus nucum (the largest and most important ligament supporting the neck). To emphasize his point, Kimi's doctor called an orthopedic surgeon into the office during one of our visits. The surgeon told us that she came very close to breaking her neck, and that if she hadn't thought to tuck just before landing, she could have been paralyzed from the fall. They restricted her from the gym for another two months.

"I don't want to go back to gymnastics," she announced in the car.

"Really?" I asked, hardly able to contain my relief if it were true. "Why not?"

"Didn't you hear what he said?" she exclaimed, "I almost broke my neck. I could be paralyzed!"

"It's just not worth that, is it?" I asked. I responded selfishly, but injuries, hospitals, physical therapy, and all the stress wore me out. I said the wrong thing because I feared for her future in this dangerous sport. This last injury dealt a devastating blow to both of us.

RESEARCH AND REFLECTION

During her eleventh year, Kimberly went from full recovery to rapid advancement and back to injury in too short a time period. The whirlwind of emotions served to magnify my dissatisfaction with gymnastics. I continued to question her development. And I continued to struggle with wanting a different way of life for our family.

In spite of her broken leg, Kimberly advanced quickly in both skills and level during her eleventh year. The injury made rapid improvement seem doubtful. However, she advanced for good reason. Between ten and twelve years old, connections in the frontal lobes of the brain develop almost as fast as they did during infancy. I remembered learning this in college. At this stage, brain growth makes girls adept at learning new skills. My daughter trained two levels in one year because it was developmentally appropriate. I found the timing advantageous for Kimi's sense of determination. Successful advancement in the face of adversity served to further encourage her passion for gymnastics.

In contrast, this year held increased dissatisfaction for me. The day that Kimberly fell on her neck tortured me as a mother beyond imagination. Before the meet, I heard mom's saying "I don't know who is more nervous, me or her." I saw about 350 gymnasts and all of their supporters, but nary a smile. You could slice the tension in the air with a knife. According to Selby and Smith comments on the sidelines at children's sporting events are 35% negative and 47% positive. I believe attitudes at a gymnastics meet seem even less positive. Sitting in support of such attitudes seemed wrong, and Kimberly's fall further emphasized my feelings of guilt.

My guilt subsided when Kimi said she didn't want to go back to gymnastics. I felt relieved because she finally shared my fear. However, our fears differed significantly. Mothering caused my fear. My daughter's fear came as a development stage in life.

After the doctor told her that she could have been paralyzed, Kimi exhibited normal fear. At age eleven or twelve, children enter into what psychologist Piaget dubbed the Formal Operation Stage. At this stage, abstraction becomes possible, which enhances problem solving abilities. This, in turn, has a dramatic effect on values, feelings, goals, emotional development and behavior. "The changing values that Piaget believed emerge as a result of formal operations may also affect the young adolescent's decisions concerning participation in movement endeavors. Because of increased idealism, the adolescent may decide that the competition common to many adolescent movement activities is not mutually beneficial to all involved and therefore opt to cease participation." (Payne and Isaacs, p. 34) Kimberly, like most girls her age, began to evaluate her own values and attitudes. According to Braselton and Greenspan, girls this age may feel caught between childhood longings and a desire to grow up. "They are fearful." (Braselton and Greenspan, p. 122)

In addition, seventy-six percent of girls aged nine to twelve say they are motivated by their mothers' influences, verses only fifty-eight percent who say they are motivated by their fathers' opinions (Selby and Smith). Looking back, I wonder if encouraging Kimberly's fear motivated her pronouncement to quit gymnastics. Her decision to quit reflected normal thought processes for a girl her age. She experienced fear and apprehension because of her age. I wonder if my fear of her sport affected her decision to quit gymnastics at this critical stage because she also wanted to share my values. I wonder how she might have reacted to the neck injury if I'd been more courageous. If only I had known what the future held... if only I had been better at sucking it up.

GET OVER IT!

"Nothing will ever be as fun as gymnastics. I miss it ...."

"Finally!" I cried out loud, as I hung up the phone.

Although I sat alone in the house, the news excited me. Kimberly's doctor released her for full activities – no restrictions. It was mid-January and two months had passed since that devastating fall. My daughter grew more restless by the day, and our homeschooling fun turned into a nightmare. Since her absence from gymnastics, we spent all of our time together. Twenty four hours a day created stress in our relationship. We both needed the doctor to release her for full activity.

Kimi already started to explore other activities. The doctor gave her permission to swim, so she spent December taking swimming lessons and trying out for synchronized swimming. We found an excellent team in a nearby city. My daughter liked the other girls, and the coach wanted to train her. The prospect thrilled me because synchronized swimming is relatively safe, it can be a lifelong sport, and the girls on her team received scholarships to some of the best colleges in the country. The transition appeared seamless and rewarding.

But, in spite of our initial excitement, water ballet turned out to be a thing of the past by mid-January. Kimberly's swimming skills needed work and she found frustration in the pool. The coach recognized potential, but my daughter didn't understand. She showed little patience for overcoming the obstacles, and couldn't develop a strong enough desire to train in the cold of winter. On the ride home one night, she sat shivering in the passenger seat.

"I hate this," she said.

"I think you need to give it more time," I responded.

"I don't want to give it more time. I don't want to swim, I don't want to be cold, and I especially don't want to be laughed at," she retorted. I thought she might cry.

"We'll talk about it again tomorrow," I answered. But she'd already made her decision. She refused to go back to the pool. I called the coach two days later, offered our gratitude and, regretfully, pulled Kimi from their training. The coach expressed both regret and understanding. We moved on to new trials.

Over the course of the next six months, Kimberly met more than ten other coaches. She tried volleyball, track, Taekwon Do, dance, softball, theater, piano, archery, and tennis. I felt caught up in a whirlwind of experimentation, and it was agonizing to watch. My daughter excelled at almost everything because gymnastics prepared her for a multitude of possibilities. Coaches sang praises to her name, and then wondered why she quit. Some asked why I let her quit. The truth is, even though she showed great potential in almost everything she attempted, she simply couldn't get excited about anything. She lost her passion and couldn't commit to anything. And I couldn't inject her with a shot of enthusiasm.

My daughter mentally withdrew. She wouldn't allow herself to get excited about anything. She transitioned from home schooling to private school in January, where she demonstrated a lack of ambition. She also behaved badly and got into trouble. Kimberly turned apathetic toward everything and angry toward almost everyone. I wondered how to help her overcome the loss of her lifelong passion. I believed she suffered from depression.

I recognized Kimberly's emotional and psychological trouble, and I couldn't help her. It knew we needed to seek professional help. We needed a sport psychologist with cross training in child psychology. I looked in the yellow pages. No luck. I called her primary care physician. No luck. I asked around. No luck. I wondered, "is there anybody out there who knows how to deal with this problem?" Finally, a friend referred me to a man who had some limited experience working with children in sports. I called him, made an appointment, and then broke the news to Kimi.

SIGNS OF DEPRESSION
Feeling sad
Chronic irritability
Fatigue
Loss of pleasure
Drop in school performance

HOW TO HELP
Take her seriously
Be direct in communicating with her
Get professional help

"Are you kidding?" she asked, followed by an emphatic, "I'm not going."

I pleaded, "Kimi, you are not doing well in school. You are angry. You cannot find a sport that you want to participate in. You need to talk to somebody about how you feel. This has been hard. I just want you to be my happy daughter again."

"I'm not going to talk to a stranger who could care less about it," she added.

I replied, "But he is a professional. He can help you sort through your options and maybe choose something that you can be happy with. He ...."

She cut me off, "I'm not going."

Great, I thought. Now what? I had time before the appointment date to persuade her, so I let it go for the time being. Two days later, following one of her outbursts, I broached the subject again.

"This is really not like you. You simply have to think about going to see the doctor. How else are you going to get better?" I launched my plea.

"Mom, I really don't want to talk about it," she responded.

"Okay, how about if you just go. You don't have to talk if you don't want to," I said.

"Sure, Mom. What kind of doctor is going to let me just sit there and not talk?" she asked.

I replied, "Just let me take care of that."

Two days later, we found a pleasant surprise at the doctor's office – a therapy dog. Kimberly loved animals, and she made friends right away. I felt optimistic. However, my optimism quickly turned to defeat. After three visits, she seemed to be making no progress whatsoever, so I questioned her.

"Kimberly, are you going to talk to the doctor?" I inquired.

"No. I already told you I didn't want to talk to a stranger about it, and he has no clue." she replied.

Wonderful, I thought. What a waste of time. What a stubborn child. What a shame. Kimi couldn't befriend the doctor as readily as she did his dog. Somehow, he failed to capture her respect and convince her that he understood the plight of a child athlete. I guessed his limited experience couldn't quite handle this situation. We moved on, and she continued to struggle.

I had a conversation with Kimi about her attitude early that summer. She decided to try spring-board diving and, although she lacked enthusiasm, she showed potential. The coach included her in a special training experience.

We had just returned from a week-long trip to Texas. I felt hopeful and one evening said to her, "You seem to like diving."

"It's okay, I guess," she responded.

It's okay? I asked myself. I just spent ten days and a bunch of money on a trip to Texas and it's *OKAY*? I was dumbfounded and not exactly thinking clearly. She was too young to care about time and money, so I paused.

Breathing a heavy sigh, I calmly asked, "What do you mean? I thought you were enjoying it."

"Nothing will ever be as fun as gymnastics. I miss it, and I've been having dreams about going back," she said.

My heart sank, because going back to gymnastics had to be the last thing I wanted. But I knew what I had to do. The next day, I talked with her about the dangers of turning away from one's passion. I provided examples of people we knew who made a decision not to pursue something they loved, even though they excelled at it. I asked her how long she would feel the regret if she didn't go back, and I told her that she should never let fear stand between her and something she wants.

Within a week, Kimberly returned to gymnastics with a smile on her face. She worked harder than I've ever seen her work. She clearly wanted to make up for lost time. I worried that she might push too hard, but I didn't say anything because she was happy. A happy Kimi enhanced family life. The house filled with her joy once again.

It was short-lived. Believe it or not, Kimberly injured herself three weeks later. She sprained her ankle, a minor injury; however, it might as well have been a broken back. My daughter suffered a crushed spirit. She did everything she could to work through the sprain, but the pain was too intense. Surprised by her claim of intense pain, I didn't know what to think. Historically, she had a high pain tolerance. However, considering all that she'd been through psychologically, I wondered whether she exaggerated this injury. Gregg and I discussed it and, after talking it over with her coaches, we decided to let her work it out for herself.

One day after practice, we took a gymnast friend of hers to visit the spring board diving practice. The coach permitted both girls to dive with the team for the day, and Kimberly left the pool complaining loudly about her injury. She claimed the pain traveled up her leg as she jumped on the spring board.

Radiated up the leg? With this new information, I decided to take my daughter for X-rays. So, the following day found us at the doctor's office … again. Within the week, we received terrible news. Kimi had a questionable spot on her bone, and it looked like it might be cancer. We made an appointment with a bone specialist. An eternity of anguish preceded that meeting.

Two days later, we sat in the waiting room at Children's Hospital. Gregg and I decided to meet with the doctor separately before taking Kimberly in to be seen. Afraid of the diagnosis and its ramifications, we thought he should know the history of her gymnastics experience. We hadn't told her about the questionable spot, and we hoped he could handle communications carefully.

Thankfully, the questionable spot on Kimi's bone turned out to be benign. I heaved a sigh of relief. However, the diagnosis did come with serious consequences. My daughter had Osteopenia – a disorder effecting bone mass which, in her case, was caused by repetitive overloading. The doctor ordered her into "retirement," a difficult concept for a twelve year old. He explained that her bones could not handle the pounding any longer. She would continue to suffer breaks and injuries. Worse, because of her age, her growth would suffer. She had to focus on growth and healing for the next four to five years.

Kimberly seemed stunned but, as usual, she refrained from crying. She spent the next few minutes listening as we discussed her diet, supplements and future development. The doctor prescribed high absorbent calcium, recommended that she avoid carbonated beverages, and emphasized the importance of bone growth. Then Kimi, being mostly concerned with the extra-curricular ramifications, asked, "Can I dance?"

"Of course you can dance," the doctor responded. "That's actually an activity that should help strengthen your bones."

As soon as we sat in the car after our visit with the doctor, Kimberly asked if she could return to ballet. Gregg and I looked at each other in disbelief. Ballet seemed the least likely of all options. Kimi tried dance during the seven-month whirlwind of experimentation with other sports. Although she showed promise, she said ballet was too slow moving for her taste. Ballet could not provide an adrenalin rush, the thing my little thrill seeker wanted most. Yet, she had natural talent that even she recognized. I remembered the summer after Kindergarten and her decision to quit ice-skating for gymnastics. She said, "God gave me more of a talent for that." I wondered if similar thinking influenced this choice. For whatever reason, my daughter returned to the dance studio within a week, and I couldn't have been happier. I liked ballet.

RESEARCH AND REFLECTION

The twelfth year is a critical age for girls. According to Brown & Gilligan, "we will mark this place as a crossroads in women's development: a meeting between girl and woman .... (p.1)" I worried about Kimberly's psychological well-being at this point. As long as she remained active, she maintained balance and self-assuredness – as do most girls. Girls in sports tend to suffer less from peer pressure because they have a greater sense of control over their lives. (Zimmerman) However, keeping my daughter involved challenged me daily. She lost her passion. I knew her self-worth up to that point came through success as a gymnast. Believing she may lose her confidence, I feared for her future. Girls with low self-esteem attempt to take control of their lives as teenagers through misguided acts with no inner direction, often resulting in self-destructive behaviors. (Zimmerman). I stayed close, and we talked a lot during this time. I had no other tool. I desperately wanted to see her happy, but I couldn't make it happen for her.

She had to work through the frustration. I could offer love, support and maybe advice – if she asked for it. Would she ask? She needed to know that she could trust me. She needed to know that I had faith in her ability to get over the disappointment and move on.

MOVING ON

Give her a goal and she'll rise to the occasion –if she wants to.

"I'm so happy to have her back!" exclaimed Kimberly's dance instructor, "You have no idea how gifted she is. She has the perfect body for dance. She was born for the ballet, not gymnastics – terribly dangerous sport."

Once again I found myself conversing with an enthusiastic coach. My demeanor must have seemed apprehensive, or in some way deserving of follow-up because after an awkward silence, she added, "Really it's quite rare that I have an opportunity to work with such potential." I flashed back to a conversation with her first gymnastics coach. It seemed so long ago.

"Well, we're just happy that she's adjusting to the end of gymnastics so well," I lied, "and we're very grateful for your patience. We know she's less enthusiastic than most of the other girls; it's been a difficult transition. You should know that Kimi asked to return to ballet immediately after the doctor told her she had to quit gymnastics. I attribute that request more to your relationship than her passion for dance at this point. Thank you."

Following that conversation, Kimberly's fondness for ballet seemed to blossom. Within a month, the studio held auditions for the Nutcracker and began a busy rehearsal schedule. Kimi developed new skills, realized that she had a knack for learning quickly, and relished the idea of being in the Christmas production. She earned several parts and, at her age, she particularly enjoyed the idea of costumes, make-up, and back stage excitement.

"I love ballet," she declared, "I never thought I would say that."

"I'm so happy for you," I responded, as we drove home after a long day of back-to-back productions.

At the same time, I thought how much more enjoyable ballet was for me. Sitting through a dance production entertained people. A gymnastics competition frazzled people. Listening to music soothed my soul. Listening to shouting, cheering, moaning, bragging, and complaining irritated me. I relaxed while watching a troupe of graceful performers dance through a storyline. I tensed up while watching a discombobulated assemblage of flipping, twisting, full throttle running, and flying through air. No more praying for safe landings. Yes, dance could easily become a welcomed addition to my mommy world. At that point, I became aware of a surprising possibility in this new setting. I could easily live vicariously through my child!

I revisited my investment in Kimberly's extra-curricular activity, and reminisced about the year that we transitioned to the more highly regarded gym. I remembered how I reacted to women who seemed to live vicariously through their daughters. I reflected on petty behaviors and attitudes that flourished in that environment. The result? Fear!

In response to my fear, I decided to watch one of Kimberly's classes in an attempt to develop a more realistic picture of her capabilities. After all, wouldn't every mother like to believe she's spawned a future prima ballerina! I knew that my maternal pride needed to be kept in check.

A week later, we headed off to dance class. On the way, Kimberly told me about an exchange she had with her instructor. "Guess what, Mom?" she asked. Without waiting for my response, she added, "Svetlana pulled me aside after the last performance and told me that I could go far as a ballerina – even farther than she did!" She seemed flattered, as she well should have been.

Wow, I thought, and speculated whether Kimberly could truly become a noteworthy ballerina. I'd heard so many different coaches and instructors praise my daughter's potential, and oftentimes I wondered about their sincerity. Quite frankly, I wondered if overstating children's potential might be a tactic to keep students enrolled in the various programs. Clearly, Kimberly had a certain degree of capability; she was a former state champion gymnast. I just didn't want her to get caught up in a false sense of reality ... again.

A healthy skepticism served me well when Svetlana approached as I watched class that afternoon. I could have easily burst at the seams as she repeated what she'd told Kimberly earlier that week, and then added, "I've wanted to move her to Pointe for a while, but I need her to attend more regularly."

"How regularly?" I inquired. Kimberly already attended three afternoons a week. I thought her dance schedule included every class possible for her level.

"I would love to work with her every day but I don't have enough classes at this time. If you can bring her four times a week, and she commits to being here for every class, I can move her to Pointe later this month."

I knew something about ballet; I'd taken it as a child. Girls don't move to Pointe that quickly. Usually it takes years of preparation. I was surprised. I asked, "Are you sure she's had enough preparation?"

Svetlana assured me, "As a former gymnast, she has unusual strength and flexibility. It usually takes dancers years to gain such ability, but she is ready."

We agreed upon a schedule, and I delivered the good news when we got into the car. Excited, Kimi wanted to go straight to the dance shop to get fitted for toe shoes. Her excitement spawned regular attendance, hard work and, predictably, a move to Pointe by the end of the month. Give her a goal and she'll rise to the occasion – if she wants to.

After Kimberly's rise to her toes, we met other highly regarded members of the dance community who believed she had great potential. The first time someone other than Svetlana recognized my daughter's potential, I heard all about it after class. Kimi got into the car acting a bit annoyed. I asked her what the problem was and she responded by blurting out, "I hate it when people try to make me the example of perfection. It's hard enough getting the other girls to be friends with me."

"What happened?" I asked.

Kimi answered, "Well, Svetlana wasn't teaching today and we had a substitute, one of the other instructors who also dances for the studio. You'd know her if you saw her. Right in the middle of class, she got down on her knees and started worshiping my feet. It was so embarrassing."

Trying to suppress my laughter as I visualized the scene, I said, "Seriously?"

"Yeah, she replied. "I was like, that's my foot. Can I have it back now? … thanks."

"Did you really say that to her?" I asked in disbelief, hoping she had better manners than that.

"No, but I was thinking it," she pouted.

The second time someone noteworthy recognized Kimberly's talent happened when the studio held its annual assessment. During the assessment, girls separate according to their ability and perform choreographed dances. Every group dances for a set of judges who evaluate each girl for the purpose of providing feedback. The staff encourages family and friends to attend, to offer practice in front of an audience. Kimberly wanted me to watch, so I did, and immediately took note of one judge that seemed to make her the focus of his attention. I couldn't exactly read his expressionless face, but I was pretty sure he liked her. The feedback that we received confirmed my suspicion, including accolades from the most critical of all judges – the man.

Perhaps the most convincing recognition we received of Kimi's potential occurred later that same year. After traveling quite a distance for school and work, Gregg and I decided to relocate our household again. As part of the relocation, we investigated the possibility of moving Kimberly to a dance studio closer to our new home. Gregg did some research and located an academy that's owned by a husband and wife team. Both danced extensively and have noteworthy credentials on the American circuit. Their dancers prepare for placement in some of the best schools and professional companies in the U.S. We decided to check it out.

When Kimberly visited the studio for observation, they asked if she had her shoes with her and if she would mind a short "audition." Having been profoundly impressed by the facility and the kind demeanor of the owner, she quickly acquiesced. At that point, Gregg and I both noted a literal jaw-dropping response to Kimi. It was clear that they wanted her in their program, and the wife even sat Kimberly down to explain how rare her gift is. She closed our encounter by promising, "Whether it is this week, next month, or next year, I would love to work with you. I have your best interest as a born dancer at heart and I hope that no matter what, you will always stick with it."

Kimberly's desire to stick with it came with recognition from one of the more advanced dancers that she had high regard for. The interaction between the two of them made a striking impact on her confidence as a future dancer. The young man, who also appeared to have a great deal of natural talent, paid special attention to her gift. He also invited her to join a small group who planned to travel for auditions to summer intensives at three of the nation's top ballet academies.

The combined effect of these experiences caused us to have greater regard for ballet. However, I feel compelled to include a caveat to our blissful new life. The transition to dance, however successful, failed to replace gymnastics in Kimberly's life. The process a young athlete must experience when separating from a serious sport is marginally recognized. Recovery involves constant uncertainty. Gymnastics required deep devotion and long term commitment. Even though she is gifted as a dancer, Kimi couldn't develop the same passion that she had for gymnastics. She continued to express grief for her loss, and I don't know if she will ever again commit herself so completely.

Committing to Kimberly's passion came with great difficulty, but the problems we faced afterward surpass every gymnastics challenge. My daughter struggled with discipline as a gymnast. But without passion, she struggles more than ever to maintain a work ethic. She learned to value hard work because of the return on her investment. She treasured the reward, making the endeavor worthwhile. Without passion, there is no reward that makes great effort meaningful. Kimi vacillates between dancing and not dancing because she cannot commit with enthusiasm. She can "suck it up" and accomplish a task, but she has yet to realize any reward.

As her mother, I continue to do the best I can in coaching her development. And I pray every day that she regains the passion for life that she had during her years as a gymnast. In the meantime, I "suck it up" and find solace in knowing she is capable of setting goals and accomplishing them. She learned the lesson that I wanted most for her to learn.

RESEARCH AND REFLECTION

During this part of the journey, I wanted Kimi to know that I loved her no matter what she chose to do. I wanted her to feel empowered, to know that she's capable of succeeding. I wanted her to know that even if her dreams didn't come true, hard work is worthwhile – it's meritorious of its own accord. My fear was that she would never again feel the passion that she felt as a gymnast. My hope was that she would learn to transfer the skills she'd learned to a new activity. And my greatest pride came in knowing that she seemed capable of finding a way to deal with her problem. I remember thinking it mature of her to reason well. At least on the surface, she recognized her pain without wallowing in it.

I also felt it important for her to develop new and strong relationships to fill the void because ".... an inner sense of connection with others is a central organizing feature of women's development and psychological crises in women's lives stem from disconnections." (Brown and Gilligan, p. 3) I encouraged new friendships at dance and school. I fostered those friendships through hosting events at home and volunteering to drive on outings.

Unfortunately, I also made a mistake during this part of the journey. Because I feared living vicariously through my daughter, I distanced myself from dance. I never wanted to encourage her for selfish reasons, because "nothing makes modern parents feel more ashamed than the awareness that what they have encouraged their children to do and be has nothing to do with the *child's best interests.*" (Swigert, p. 104) According to Selby and Smith, absent or excessive involvement is related to stress, moderation is related to enjoyment. Kimberly's stress reflected my emotional distance during the dance years.

However, on a more positive note, at twelve years, the brain "prunes" itself of excess gray matter, focusing on areas most often utilized. For this reason, activities that have been practiced most during this time will tend to reappear later in life. (Gurian) Kimi practiced dance at the age of twelve and discovered a life-long activity even in the absence of passion.

INDECISION

....being a mom meant forcing Kimberly to do things she usually wanted to do on her own.

"I love ballet," Kimi told me as she got into the car. "Sometimes I just don't want to go. It's kind of like the bathtub. You never want to get in, but once you're in, you never want to get out. I'm sorry about before class."

I reluctantly argued with her before class because of her indecisiveness towards dance. She asked if she had to go, and I felt torn. I did not want to be the decision maker. It was her activity, not mine. I only wanted to drive her to and fro, write the checks and provide moral support. My list of things to do didn't include forcing her to attend class. However, I knew that she both wanted to go and didn't want to go.

I knew my daughter better than she knew herself. She had a positive attitude about almost everything, and she stayed on task if she was in a good mood. On a bad day, she would refuse a trip to Disneyland. On those days, getting her out of bed seemed to be a big accomplishment. And I forced myself to be the mom I never had to be with her before. I forced myself to be the mom I hated to be.

On a bad day, being a mom meant forcing Kimberly to do things she usually wanted to do on her own. I trusted those things included dance, especially considering the benefit of a fresh outlook at the end of class. I had to plan our days with this in mind. I despised those days, and so did she. On those days she secretly questioned her existence. She became existential. She wondered if I was forcing her to perform because I wanted to live vicariously through her. She'd seen it before, and she knew I valued dance more than gymnastics. My heart ached for her. And it ached for me. I seemed to be the woman I loathed in myself – the woman I never wanted to become. In her eyes, at least, I was that woman. I felt the worst of the worst in my history of sucking it up.

Kimberly was almost fourteen years old. Emotionally, she hit rock bottom. My daughter lost touch with herself – her ambition and her zest for life. She completely forgot about the support system that she had to draw upon. She withdrew, turning her back on life, love and anything that held meaning in her prior years. She started making poor choices – socially, educationally and personally. Kimi floundered, seemed overly concerned about peer pressure, and generally lost control of her life after gymnastics. She was like a clam with me, opening up to expel dirt or take in nourishment. I had to wait around for an opportunity to present itself if I wanted to offer guidance. It was a precarious time.

My daughter's depression worsened as she entered High School. She experienced a significant drop in performance and developed chronic irritability. She lost interest in almost everything and showed signs of fatigue. My happy-go-lucky little girl just didn't care about much of anything anymore. It seemed she'd run out of steam. At that point she recognized in herself an inability to suck it up, and she asked for help. We sought the support of a professional.

It took a year of therapy, medication, understanding teachers, and a compassionate dance instructor to stabilize my daughter. Kimberly got back on track, expressing a desire to participate in the things she enjoys, and making healthy choices. She still vacillated, and indecision controlled her thoughts, but she forged ahead. And on a bad day, she leaned on me for support.

"I want to do better, I want to because I want to, not because it is surprising to the human soul that I, Kimberly Casey Coad, would attend the road to failure. I have always been the one with the <u>potential</u>. Well it's my potential and I will do what I want with it. I should not be strained to change my appearance or my schedule for something that has not been mine. It was yours, you missed out, God gave you other gifts, let me have mine. Let me have mine for me, let me use the gifts he has given me to honor Him, and make HIM happy. Not for your own personal abuse, so you can use my potential. He gave them to me, knowing that I would carry on exactly what I will with them. I have <u>talent</u>; I have <u>potential</u>, what is the point? What will I do with this "potential" if I don't know the purpose? Is this even what I want? Do I even know what I want? Someone who will hold the door open for others to follow? Not someone who is absorbed in their own functions, someone that will perjure through their teeth to get what they yearn for? My way is so <u>effortless</u>. I get what I want when I want. But is that even what I really ache? Do I wish for that kind of a lifestyle? I'm sorry, I'm sorry I disappoint you. I'm sorry that I'm not your little shinning <u>star</u>, someone who will never make a difference in the world besides on stage. You tell me, you tell me to do my best and follow <u>my</u> dreams, <u>my</u> goals. Is that correct? Is that what I am to do? I don't want to be the family sketch. I want to be a girl, a girl who has potential and talent. Talents to do <u>anything</u> I please, not anything you please. I look in the mirror admiring myself some days and loathing myself others. I don't want to be judged, to be traded like cattle, and trained like a dog. Why must I use these anonymous "talents"? Why do I even have them? Why me? Why always me? I weary with this routine. I will perform it; I will not open my trap and pose these questions. I will be your up-and-comer and never have a life to posses. Never have something for <u>myself</u>; never be what I yearn for, instead be what you want me to be. I will <u>hush up</u>, entomb myself and carry on my life as if all this was a fantasy. As if I had never even asked these questions to myself, as if it had never even intersected my mind."

RESEARCH AND REFLECTION

According to Walters, Mothers and daughters come to understand their relationships with each other through family experience, cultural influences and social construct. In today's culture, we are quick to blame the unloving or over-loving mother for their daughters' neuroses and unhappiness. "Mothers and mothering are central in this new dialog of female angst ....tellingly point to our mothers as setting the stage for our tendency to love too much ....or our inability to recognize that we can never have it all." (Walters, p. 7)

I have to admit, I wonder if I loved Kimberly enough – or too much. I question myself and my competency. I have reservations about whether I may be at least partially responsible for her angst. I doubt if I remembered to teach her that she cannot have it all, and I am certain that I allowed her to be exposed to cultural influences that run contrary to my values.

On the other hand, "daughters can derive enormous benefits from mothers who allow them to live their own lives with maximal maternal support and minimal interference." (Walters, p. 225) I know for certain this has been my goal all along. Have I accomplished that goal?

In what ways has her psyche been affected by my mothering? Do I analyze the experience too deeply? Could I have done it better? These are questions most mothers ask themselves. "What is most denied about child rearing is the altruism required and how draining it can be to constantly give care, protection, and empathy. We seem to be most reluctant to examine the spectrum of emotions evoked when we give time, attention, understanding, and compassion to someone who cannot really return these gifts, at least not for a long time." (Swigert, p. 103) What have I received in return for the altruistic love I have for my daughter? A most humanizing experience, at the very least.

WHAT NEXT?

I attribute her bravery to gymnastics.

What next? That's a funny question considering the roller coaster ride we've been on. Kimberly continues to suffer the heartache of her loss, and she says she doesn't think she will ever be healed. "I'll never find anything to love as much as I love gymnastics," are her exact words. My daughter still dreams about gymnastics and devises schemes for returning to the sport. However, reality brings her to the same conclusion each time: she is too old to accomplish the goal that she had as a gymnast. She is also too competitive to settle for less than the pursuit of that goal. Regardless of her residual passion, Kimi refuses to set herself up for what she believes would become an even greater heartache.

Yet she fears she might never find something to surrender herself to, something she *wants* to devote her life to with that familiar passion. She says she's past the age where coaches tell her she can do it. When we talk, she expresses the following sentiment:

"I dream all these dreams of sticking with dance for a straight year. But they are just dreams, and I am setting myself up for failure and heartbreak to think differently. Goal is a foreign word to me now. My goals are gone. The only goal that ever mattered is gone. I'll never get over it mom, never. I already had my fifteen minutes of fame, and I need to focus on reality now."

Kimberly recently applied for a job as a coach, but decided not to pursue it. She could not witness, or even guide others to success without pain. For her, participation is the only option. She continues to dance, and has performed in Swan Lake along with subsequent productions of the Nutcracker. She's earned solo parts, and loves to be on stage. However, she continues to run hot and cold in her desire to dance.

My daughter is away at college now, where she also finds joy in writing.

Her writing takes shape in the form of fantasy, as she has a vivid imagination and a wide vocabulary. Perhaps writing is her catharsis, but maybe it's her new challenge. Regardless, of the reason, I am thankful. I'm glad that she's learned to get out of bed each morning and, for the most part, approach each day with fresh optimism. I attribute her bravery to gymnastics. Female athletes have a greater sense of power and self-esteem that leads them to take on challenges as they mature. (Zimmerman)

RESEARCH AND REFLECTION

I try not to be too quick to interfere in my daughter's life at this point. Through our journey, I've learned the strength of her spirit. Life with her is full of surprises. The upcoming phases will surely bring more unexpected events. In the meantime, as I continue with daily life, I hope that I might benefit from the wisdom of the Jungian writer Irene Claremont de Castellejo:

> "Parents ... tend to see the defects and to believe the complexities of their children; but if they are wise they will remember that they do *not* know the innermost truth of their children's souls. We do *not* know the destiny to which another has been born. We do not know where he is to rebel, which mistakes he is to make. Perhaps some idiosyncrasy or some failure to fit into society may be that child's particular contribution to the world, which should not be cured but fostered. We may see the mistakes of the young but if we are wise we must also learn to be blind; to know and yet *not* to know is one of the paradoxical secrets of relationships." (Bassoff, p. 75)

According to Christiane Northrup (2005), words are powerful and, used in a positive way, allow Kimi to use her own energy towards healing. I believe in realistic communication, positive messages and genuine compassion. Kimberly understands that I have faith in her abilities, and she calls regularly for advice. She is mastery oriented and understands well that it is her own effort over time that produces results. I believe she learned the importance of attitude. "As she struggles with problems, teach her about attitude. Attitude can make or break a situation, turning it from disaster to a great learning experience." (Gedeberg, p. 117)

My daughter, like everyone else, has frustrations. She tends to be hard on herself, but I'm satisfied with her accomplishments. I often remind her of the progress that she's made. We attribute her sense of self-worth to the experiences she had as a gymnast. I hope Kimi finds adventure and a direction in college. I pray that she continues to select appropriate challenges. But mostly, I await the day when she finds renewed passion.

MOTHERS AS MENTORS
People see themselves as they believe others see them – labels and expectations should give the message that you see girls as capable, competent and resilient
Advise and help select appropriate challenges – those that don't make her feel overwhelmed, or are unrealistic
Avoid exhaustion and/or a tyrannical approach – show satisfaction with her performance
Allow your daughter to broaden her vision, even find ways to encourage such behavior
Motivate her interest and capture her attention through adventure
Remind her of the progress she makes along the way
Avoid negative judgments, use positive requests regarding expectations instead
Avoid sarcasm, it devalues the recipient
Never use clarifying questions (i.e., Why?), it elicits excuses
Remember: People Compare Themselves to Others – both individuals and groups
Help her understand the concept of Learned Helplessness – a lack of effort does not equal outcome (learned helplessness produces a negative self-concept, resulting in a lack of responsibility)
Teach Mastery – help her realize that effort over time results in outcome (mastery produces a positive self-concept, resulting in a sense of responsibility)

AFTERWARD

Since the writing of this book, Kimberly has continued to grow and so have I. Upon reflection of our journey into and out of gymnastics, I wonder most about the role passion plays in our life. I contemplate my parenting choices in response to her passion. I question the value of my own training and experience in the fields of human development, psychology and education. And I ask myself if there is an answer to any of these questions. After all, life is a journey regardless of where it takes you. Parenting is a journey regardless of how well prepared one thinks she is. And, at least in this country, life without passion is not something we strive for. The American culture values achievement, the pursuit of happiness and, above all else, passion along the way.

The question of why Kimberly's passion was so important gave me pause. I encouraged her passion for so long that the rationale escaped me. Why was her passion important? Why do some parents encourage their children's passions and what drives the decisions of those who don't? I'm not sure if there is a single answer, except that our values and culture drive our behavior. When the media highlights any high achiever, they often include an investigation of the achiever's childhood. They interview parents, teachers and other influential people such as coaches. Parenting classes teach us to raise our children "right," meaning we should do everything in our power to contribute to society through our offspring. Educators are trained to teach children how to perform to the best of their ability – to function in a competitive world. Coaches who produce winning athletes are labeled "good coaches."

I also considered the element of personal values. It's true that some parents encourage their children's passions and some don't – regardless of societal influences. I believe this difference reflects personal values. Parents who encourage, or even simply permit, their children to pursue a dangerous sport value life differently than parents who forbid it. Parents who encourage or permit dangerous activities probably value the enjoyment of life more than life itself. A parent who forbids dangerous activities values life first, and the enjoyment of life second. Parents who deny the pursuit of passion may tend to follow a more traveled path in life, expecting familiar outcomes. The parent who allows her child to pursue a passion probably cares less about risk and may be more willing to gamble with the outcome. I believe such individuals tend to be more pioneering – a spirit this country was founded on.

So in keeping with my own pioneering spirit, I permitted my daughter to pursue her passion. I even encouraged it when it got difficult. And, as an educator and human development specialist, I believed I was well prepared to parent her through the journey. Yet, the journey tortured me, and I reflect upon the experience with wonder – a tinge of regret even. I look back on instances where my training and education should have been more useful. In my own mind I knew the answers to questions that arose during those times. But my emotions got in the way. On more than one occasion, I failed to harness my own feelings in her best interest. Many times the Developmental Theory came to bear just a bit too late.

Personally, I underwent developmental phases of my own during the gymnastics years. Life is fluid, ever changing and unpredictable. As a mother, I learned that lesson in a very real way. Even with my education, training and experience, motherhood is the greatest challenge I've ever faced. Regardless of her ability, talent and passion, gymnastics was the greatest challenge I could help Kimi face. The journey taught me to appreciate experience and motherhood above education and training. Don't misunderstand. Education and training are highly valuable assets in life. Without them I couldn't have been employed. Without education, I would understand the trek and reflect on it less. Without training, I would never have this opportunity to share my perspective. My personal passion is to help other parents guide children through sports. Without education and training, my passion could not become a goal.

Yet, without the experience of mothering Kimi through the gymnastics years, I would have even less reasons to be grateful. The child who developed through it all brings joy to my life. The constant surprises that accompany parenthood keep life interesting. Parenting and sharing experiences are the reason I write. Education and training just give me the tools.

So, the answer to the question about Kimi's passion and why I encouraged it is simply a matter of personal values and cultural influences. I believe in the American Dream and the pursuit of happiness. I honestly believed the experience had more value than the opportunity it presented. Through my experience, I've learned to see the journey itself as a success. Regardless of whether a particular goal is accomplished, life's journey is a thing to treasure.

BIBLIOGRAPHY

Brown and Gilligan. *Meeting at the Crossroads; Women's Psychology and Girls' Development.*

Chesler, Phyllis. *Woman's Inhumanity to Woman.*

Cogan, Karen, Silver Bernstein and Peter Vidmar. *Sport Psychology Library Gymnastics.*

Douglas, Susan and Meredith W. Michaels. (2004). *The Mommy Myth; The Idealization of Motherhood and How it Has Undermined Women.* New York: New York Free Press.

Gadeberg, Jeanette. *Raising Strong Daughters.*

Galton, Lawrence. (1980). *Your Child in Sports; A Complete Guide.* New York: Franklin Watts.

Gurian, Michael. (2002). *The Wonder of Girls; Understanding the Hidden Nature of Our Daughters.* New York. Pocket Books.

Maine, Margo PhD. D. *Body Wars; Making Peace With Women's Bodies.*

Marone, Nicky. (1998). *How to Mother a Successful Daughter; A Practical Guide to Empowering Girls from Birth to Eighteen.* New York. Harmony Books.

Missieroglu, Gina. *Girls Like Us.*

Northrup, Christiane, M.D. (2005). *Mother-Daughter Wisdom; Creating a Legacy of Physical and Emotional Health.* New York. Bantam Books.

Payne, V. Gregory and Larry D. Isaacs. (1995). *Human Motor Development; a Lifespan Approach.* Mountain View, California: Mayfield Publishing Company.

Saline, Carol and Sharon J. Wohlmuth. *Mothers & Daughters.*

Silby, Caroline, PhD. D. and Shelley Smith. (2000). *Games Girls Play; Understanding and Guiding Young Female Athletes.* New York: St. Martin's Press.

Swigart, Jane, PhD. (1998). *The Myth of the Perfect Mother.* Chicago: Il. Contemporary Books.

Walters, Suzanna Danuta. (1978). *Lives Together Worlds Apart; Mothers and Daughters in Popular Culture.* Los Angeles: University of California Press.

Warner, Judith. *Perfect Madness; Motherhood in the Age of Anxiety.*

Wiseman, Rosalind. (2006). *Queen Bee Moms and King Pin Dads.* New York. Crown Publishers.

Zimmerman, Jean and Gil Reavill. (1998). *Raising Our Athletic Daughters.* New York: Doubleday.

16254596R00062

Made in the USA
Lexington, KY
14 July 2012